The Waveney Lifeboats

An illustrated history of the RNLI 44ft Waveney lifeboats 1967–1999

Nicholas Leach

© Nicholas Leach 2001

All rights reserved. Nicholas Leach is hereby identified as the author of this work in accordance with Section 77 of the Copyright, Designs and Patents Act 1988.

ISBN 1-902953-01-0
Published by Bernard McCall, 'Halia', 400 Nore Road, Portishead, Bristol BS20 8EZ
Printed by Dalton Printers, Thesiger Street, Cathays, Cardiff CF24 4BN

Cover   *Thomas James King* (44-013) off Barns Ness lighthouse, south of Dunbar, in 1995. (Rick Tomlinson)

Back cover   One of the last Waveneys built by the RNLI, *John Fison* (44-020), passing Lowestoft harbour in 1998. (Nicholas Leach)

Above   The first Waveney built for the RNLI, *John F Kennedy* (44-002), which served at Dun Laoghaire. (RNLI)

Acknowledgements

The 44ft Waveney has international origins, and therefore my gratitude extends to people throughout the world, particularly in the United States where Scott Price, Dennis Noble, Robert Witter and Gerard Dutton provided help and assistance. William D Wilkinson freely offered advice and supplied many photographs for which I am deeply grateful. In Canada, Clay Evans of the Canadian Coast Guard provided help and information. The website maintained by Clive Lawford was consulted regularly, and Clive's work is highly recommended to all interested in the 44ft motor lifeboats. At the RNLI Headquarters in Poole, Edward Wake-Walker, Jon Jones, Derek King and Barry Cox have all been of assistance; I owe a large debt of gratitude to Derek Scrivener, of RNLI Service Information, who supplied much information without which it would have been impossible to produce this book; the records of the late Grahame Farr, held in the RNLI's library, were also consulted. For help with the draft versions, thanks to Paul Russell; for providing additional information, thanks to Jeff Morris in particular and also Steve

Renyard. For very kindly supplying photographs for possible inclusion, I am most grateful to Paul Arro, Hull; Thomas Brown, Troon; John Buckby, Poole; Brian Chandler, Hexham; Tony Denton, Shrewsbury; Steve Dutton, Stockton-on-Tees; Peter Edey, Brightlingsea; David Gooch, Houghton Regis; Ian Johnson, Troon; Clive Lawford; Mrs Hattie Lee, Falkland Islands; Gary Markham, Gorleston; John Markham, Gorleston; Justin Merrigan, Tasmania; Ian Moignard, Jersey; Tony Moore, Redcar; Jeff Morris, Coventry; Paul Russell, Hitchin; Rick Tomlinson; Colin Watson, Banbridge; Phil Weeks, Chatham; and Bob Williams, Hartlepool. In New Zealand, the following provided information and photographs: Harold Mason, Immediate Past President of the Royal New Zealand Coastguard Federation and Convenor of the Waveney Project; John Jamieson, of Mana Coastguard; Richard Craig; Sue Landers; and John Gower, of Raglan Coastguard. Finally, on a personal note, my thanks to Sarah for her patience, understanding and companionship during the writing and preparation of this book.

The Waveney Lifeboats

An illustrated history of the RNLI 44ft Waveney lifeboats 1967-1999

Contents

United States Coast Guard 44ft motor lifeboat CG-44347.
(Official USCG photo)

Development of the 44ft motor lifeboat

In July 1999 the last 44ft Waveney class lifeboat was taken out of service by the Royal National Lifeboat Institution. For more than a quarter of a century, Waveneys had been in service throughout the United Kingdom and Republic of Ireland, and given outstanding service performing many rescues. This book is a tribute to this outstanding and ground-breaking design of lifeboat.

This introductory section is a background history to the design, development and construction of the 44ft motor lifeboats introduced in the United States in the early 1960s, built for the United States Coast Guard to carry out search and rescue work under heavy sea and surf conditions. Such was the outstanding nature of this design that boats built to it served not only in the United States but also in the United Kingdom and Ireland, and in Canada, Portugal, Norway, Italy and Iran. This book details specifically the design as used by the Royal National Lifeboat Institution in the United Kingdom and Ireland where it was known as the Waveney class lifeboat. The design was the first 'fast lifeboat' to see service in British waters and as such represents the beginning of the modern lifeboat era. The worldwide influence on lifeboat development of the 44ft motor lifeboat is testament to its outstanding design and build quality which provided seaworthiness, ease of handling, speed, strength and durability that was second to none. It probably represents the most significant advance in lifeboat design of the 20th century.

Motor lifeboats in the United States

The first motor lifeboat to see service in the USA, a standard 34ft self-righting lifeboat fitted with a 12hp petrol engine, was trialled by the United States Life-saving Service (USLSS) in 1899. The success of this boat led to many other 34ft lifeboats being so converted. Improvements in engine technology continued and in 1907 the first lifeboat designed from the keel up as a motor lifeboat entered service.

At this time the Coast Guard as it is today did not exist. It came into existence in 1915 when the USLSS was merged with the US Revenue Cutter Service, and the new service became fully responsible for search and rescue off America's seaboard. Although law enforcement operations were also part of the organisation's remit, a large network of lifeboat stations, known as 'units', was maintained for rescue work.

The newly-created United States Coast Guard continued developing motor lifeboats where the USLSS had left off. Its first new motor lifeboat, the Type H, was first built in 1918. Further new designs were introduced in 1928 and in 1937 the Type TRS was first built. This 36ft 8in self-bailing and self-righting single-engined craft became the mainstay of the USCG lifeboat fleet until production ceased in 1956.

The 36-footers, as they were known, were fitted with a single 100hp petrol engine which gave a speed of almost 10 knots and a cruising radius of about 200 miles. Most were kept afloat, although some were carriage launched and kept in a boathouse. USCG personnel reached a high degree of efficiency in handling this lifeboat, which proved its worth in many rescues both on the seacoasts and in the Great Lakes and was the workhorse of the service for many years. However, by the 1960s, a decade which began with 150 boats of this type in service, the design was beginning to show its age. The boats themselves had an average age of 19 years, and they were showing definite signs of wear.

Not only was the 36-footer showing its age, but it was no longer meeting the operational requirements of the USCG. Recreational boating in the United States had increased considerably during the 1950s, and the country's coastal waters had become densely populated with a variety of small craft. When the weather worsened, recreational boaters and small commercial fishermen were getting into trouble. As speed was crucial in reaching these casualties, a 40ft utility boat, capable of 21 knots, entered service to supplement the 36-footer and provide routine assistance in fair weather. In rough weather, however, the 36-footer was called upon. Consequently many stations had to operate two vessels, an unnecessary expense, particularly when one of these boats, the slow 36-footer, was poorly suited to the high volume of work it had to undertake. A new design of faster, all-weather craft was needed which could perform the roles of both the 40ft and the 36ft craft.

To develop a new design, it was necessary to ascertain the characteristics to be incorporated. The main operational shortcomings of the 36-footers were identified as poor towing control due to the far aft location of the tow bitt, lack of speed, and poor visibility at the steering position. However, the design had its strengths and the crews who operated the boats stressed these must be kept. In designing a new boat,

The standard 36ft USCG lifeboat, seen here with an open aft cockpit, had a relatively limited speed. (Official USCG photo)

This photo of the 36-footer shows the displacement hull shape, with aft cockpit partially enclosed. (Official USCG photo)

seaworthiness, self-righting capability and compartmentation, all strengths of the 36-footer, could not be compromised.

The new design had to be both fast and able to operate in the worst of weathers. It also had to have a full electronic configuration to include radar, automatic direction finder, depth finder and radio. In addition, it had to have twin screws, a range of 150 nautical miles at full speed, provisions for survivors, engine-driven fire and salvage pump, excellent towing capability and an integrated steering and control console.

Comparison of characteristics		
	36-footer	**44-footer**
Length	36ft 8in	44ft 1in
Beam OA	10ft 8in	12ft 8in
Power	90-100hp (single)	360hp (twin)
Speed	10 knots (est)	12-15 knots (est)
Displacement	8.9 tons	14.2 tons

Development of the 44ft motor lifeboat

Once the requirements of the new design had been ascertained, a USCG design team produced lines for a motor lifeboat to meet these requirements. The characteristics of the new motor lifeboat evolved in July 1960 and a preliminary design was prepared for model tank testing. Self-righting was achieved by the fundamental design which combined a lightweight superstructure with a low centre of gravity and hull compartmentation. A 1:12 scale model was constructed from the plans and subjected to resistance and trim tests at the experimental tank of Davidson Laboratory at the Stevens Institute of Technology. This was the first time that a lifeboat design had been model-tested prior to the building of a prototype. Technology had advanced sufficiently to enable the designers to rely on tests with the model, and thus reduce the number of problems, both inevitable and costly, that would appear in a full-scale boat.

The design of the new lifeboat was found to meet the criteria specified. The ability to operate in coastal waters under unusually severe weather and sea conditions was achieved, and the boat fulfilled its seaworthiness requirement. It was able to make progress into head seas at speed without causing damage to the boat's structure or equipment, and without physically punishing the crew. The

hull was constructed to combine maximum strength with minimum weight. The boat not only had to survive severe conditions at sea, but also had to be able to take the ground, work in heavy surf, and tow vessels while be light enough to achieve a reasonably good speed.

The hull was constructed from welded Corten steel, a special low carbon formulation possessing high strength and corrosion-resisting properties which gave ease of hull maintenance. The bulkheads, hull framing, raised decks and cockpit deck were all constructed of mild steel. To protect the vessel against possible damage should it be grounded, a double bottom was provided in the forward half-length of the boat, and a strong keel extended aft. The hull was further divided into seven watertight compartments, framed by a combination of transverse and longitudinal bulkheads. The compartments consisted of cable locker, forward cabin, crew's cabin, engine room, void compartment, after cabin and steering gear compartment.

The open wheelhouse incorporated an adjustable seat for the helmsman and Morse single lever speed and gearbox controls for operating the main engines. The steering position was also equipped with starting controls, an instrument panel, a compass and remote-operated electronic equipment. Survivor accommodation consisted of seating for

An artists impression of the 44ft motor lifeboat for service with the United States Coast Guard before the design was finalised. Note the open wheelhouse and mast with minimal electronic aids. The idea for an open steering position was probably carried over from the 36-footer, but with a greater speed, the 44-footer would need much better crew protection. (Official USCG photo)

USCG diagram of the standard 44-footer as built and used in service. The design incorporated a rounded-bottom hull which had an overall length of 44ft 1in, breadth of 12ft 8in and draft of 3ft 2in. The boat had a full load displacement of 41,500lbs and a normal operating displacement of 35,360lbs.

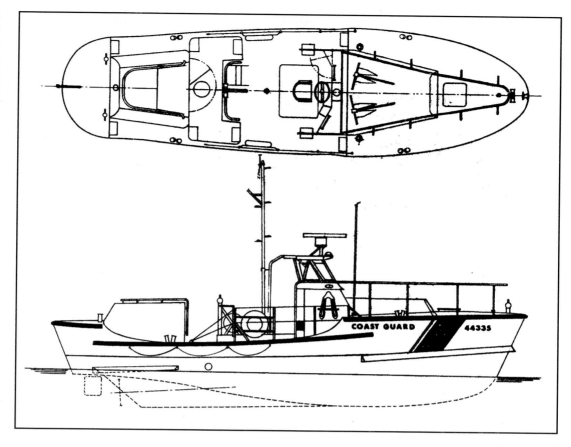

ten persons, together with a small galley and toilet. There was also stowage space for basic fire-fighting equipment. Towing equipment consisted of a tow bitt 4-inches in diameter and tow line stowage reel with 100 fathoms of 3½-inch circumference nylon rope.

Power was provided by two 180hp diesel engines driving twin three-bladed bronze propellers. The port engine was also used to drive the fire and salvage pump, as well as the hydraulic system to start the main engines. The starboard engine powered the hydraulic steering system pump. After trials of the prototype, stern fins were added just below the water line on either side of the hull to improve the trim of the boat, together with foil rudders and power-assisted steering. These modifications greatly enhanced control of the boat and its operation in following seas.

Construction for the USCG

Construction of a prototype boat began at the Coast Guard Yard at Baltimore in April 1961 and this was completed in 1962. Designated CG-44300, the new craft was launched in February 1962 and subjected to rough water testing on the Atlantic Coast as the first part of an extended and exhaustive evaluation programme. After initial rough water testing, CG-44300 left the CG Yard on 14 April 1962 and visiting a number of lifeboat stations along the East coast during passage from Hatteras Inlet to Maine, before going on operational duty at Chatham Station, Massachusetts. In October 1962 the boat left Chatham and arrived in Seattle, Washington, on 19 October, for evaluation by the 13th Coast Guard District on the north-western seaboard.

During early November the boat was tested on the bar at

Yaquina Bay, Oregon, in the heavy breaking surf conditions typical of this part of the Pacific Northwest coast. During the rough-water evaluation, CG-44300 was repeatedly taken into the breaking seas on the bar and a nearby reef. With Giles Vanderhoof, a Chief Boatswain's Mate of the USCG, in command, the boat was taken head on into the waves. Vanderhoof also turned the stern of the boat to the waves, and let the craft be hurled by the force of the seas. Frequently the boat was lifted entirely clear of the water by the breaking seas. Although the impact on its return to the bottom of the intervening trough was considerable, the hull and equipment remained intact.

The top of the boat's mast was just over 20ft above the waterline, and the height of the waves was considerably greater than this. Vanderhoof deliberately broached the boat, an almost fatal manoeuvre for small boats, and the breaking seas that engulfed the boat smashed the windscreen on more than one occasion, but the boat survived. Various items, such as the glass in the windscreen, needed strengthening as a result of the trials, but overall the boat surpassed the expectations of the trials team. Under conditions ranging from large ground swells offshore to short ebb waves, moderate breaking seas and large dangerous seas on bars and reefs, CG-44300 gave excellent performance and admirably survived the trials.

One of the more important design criteria for the 44ft boat was an ability to manoeuvre in the surf, proved during the trials. In taking large breaking seas bow on, considerable power could be used to carry the boat to the top of the wave to avoid broaching or pitch-poling. Then, just as the bow passed through the top of the break, the power was throttled

Capsizing and righting trials of CG-44300

The self-righting characteristics of the 44ft boat were tested during capsizing trials. During these trials the boat righted in four to six seconds, depending on whether the fuel tanks were full or empty. These photos show the prototype 44-footer CG-44300 being capsized at the USCG yard, Curtis Bay, Maryland on 28 September 1961. (Official USCG photos, courtesy of William Wilkinson)

CG-44300: history

CG-44300 was the prototype 44ft motor lifeboat. During her operational career with the USCG, she served at Station Yaquina Bay from October 1962 until 1981. In July 1981 she was transferred to the National Motor Lifeboat School at Cape Disappointment, Washington, where she served for a further 15 years. Since 1996 she has been displayed at the Columbia River Maritime Museum.

CG-44300: specifications

Length overall	44ft 1½in
Length waterline	40ft
Beam overall	12ft 8in
Beam waterline	10ft 10in
Draft	3ft 2½in
Displacement	15.8 tons
Fuel capacity	333 gallons
Water capacity	16 gallons
Shaft horsepower	Maximum 400
Trial speed	15.3 knots
Endurance	200 miles at 10 knots
	150 miles at 15 knots
Range of stability	In excess of 175 degrees
Engines	Twin GM 6V-53 diesels
Engines (production boats)	Twin Cummins V6-200

The prototype 44-footer, CG-44300, was completed in 1962, and is seen here during her trials. The new design gained almost instant approval from the crews who tested her. (Official USCG photos, from the collection of William Wilkinson)

back and headway lost, so the boat slid down the back of the wave with no pounding experienced. The twin screws, twin rudders and power steering, gave the boat an excellent level of manoeuvrability. In the hands of an experienced and skilled Coxswain, she could be turned 180 degrees between the crests of two breaking seas, an invaluable capability when taking people from the water in surf conditions. Various modifications were made as a result of experiences gained from the evaluation trials, but overall the requirements laid out for the new 44ft design had been fulfilled in the new boat.

During this period CG-44300 cruised approximately 3000 miles at an average speed of 11.1 knots with an overall fuel rate of 20.4 gallons per hour. The boat proved capable of operating up to 50 miles offshore, in surf conditions up to 20 feet, seas up to 30 feet, winds up to 50 knots, and of towing vessels up to 125 gross tons. Its first serious rescue took place in December 1962 when, in a south-westerly gale, a 150ft-long barge was towed for approximately three hours, a

distance of 8 miles in seas up to 15ft in height.

In summary, the outstanding features of the design were identified as follows: strong rudder action and power steering enabling manoeuvres to be quickly executed; exceptional hull design enabling the boat to negotiate large breaking seas and run into large seas without excessive pounding; crew comfort and safety afforded by good sea-keeping, berthing, padded interiors and adequate compartment heat; a covered helm station which afforded good shelter for the helmsmen; towing bitt and hawser arrangement enabling one person to work the towline hook-up; and hull construction and corrosion protection systems.

Lieutenant Commander Robert Witter, Chief of the USCG Boat Section, stated that "the all-weather capabilities evidenced throughout this comprehensive development project are considered to rank the USCG 44ft motor lifeboat as one of the finest rescue craft of its type in the world." The new design was ready to enter service.

In September 1961, Commandant of the Coast Guard,

Diagrams taken from the USCG 44' MLB Type Manual which show some of the equipment used on the USCG's 44-footers.

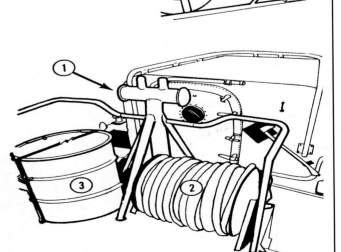

The nylon dodger foul weather curtain attached to the aft portion of the wheelhouse roof helped to protect the coxswain should a wave break over the boat.

(1) Searchlight; (2) Air horn; (3) Blue light; (4) Radar Antenna; (5) Mast; (6) FM Antenna; (7) FM homer antennas; (8) AM Antenna; (9) 60lb Danforth anchor; (10) 28lb Danforth anchor; (11) Bull nose; (12) Forward mooring bitt; (13) Anchor line hause pipe.

The pump (3), towing bitt (1) and tow reel (2) working area, situated aft of the coxswain's position. The midship position of the towing bitt helped to give the 44-footer an excellent towing capability.

Admiral A. C. Richmond, announced that new 44ft lifeboats would replace 36-footers at the rate of about 10 per year. On 9 March 1962, CG Headquarters announced that CG-44300 was to be the prototype for an 18-boat construction programme, later expanded to 25 boats, designated CG-44301 to CG-44324. The intention was to build 100 44-footers for CG rescue stations on the Atlantic Coast from Cape Hatteras north, on the Pacific Coast from San Francisco north, and on the Great Lakes.

A total of 110 were eventually constructed, of which 106 entered service with the US Coast Guard, while the remaining four were sold for use abroad. All were constructed at the USCG Yard at Curtis Bay on the Chesapeake River, where one 44-footer could be completed and be ready for delivery into service in approximately six months. The boats built in the first construction programme of the 1960s cost on average £115,000, while the last boat, CG-44409, completed in 1972, cost £225,000. By the 1980s 105 boats were in active service, operating from 77 stations along the Atlantic and Pacific coasts and the Great Lakes.

After the trial programme had ended, CG-44300 continued in service and between October 1962 and 1981 served at Station Yaquina Bay. In July 1981 she was transferred to the National Motor Lifeboat School at Cape Disappointment, Washington, where she served for a further 15 years. The boat was involved in strenuous duties at all times, going end-over-end and rolling completely several times. However, she was always up to the task, and won the admiration and affection of her crews, training coxswains and operators from stations throughout the US. The 44-footer became the Coast Guard's standard heavy weather and surf rescue response platform, capable of effecting a rescue at sea under the most difficult circumstances. The outstanding design proved to be almost unsinkable and gained great popularity with Coast Guardsmen.

Interest from the RNLI

When the RNLI began to show an interest in the USCG 44ft motor lifeboat in 1963, it was the first time the Institution had seriously considered putting a fast lifeboat into service on a nationwide basis. Although a fast lifeboat, 64ft in length and named *Sir William Hillary* (ON.725), had been built n 1929 for service at Dover, this was a one-off craft. Designed to help ditched aircraft in the English Channel, she was powered by twin 375hp engines and could reach speeds of more than 17 knots. When she was taken over by the Admiralty in October 1940, the RNLI did not operate any more fast lifeboats until after World War II.

Top CG-44303 takes a heavy breaker head-on at the mouth of the Umpqua River, Oregon, in conditions typical of the American seaboard. (Official USCG photo)

Middle Although primarily used for search and rescue tasks as illustrated here, 44-footers were also used for law enforcement and other general duties. (Official USCG photo)

Bottom CG-44385 in standard USCG livery. (Official USCG photo)

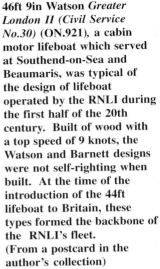

46ft 9in Watson *Greater London II (Civil Service No.30) (ON.921)*, a cabin motor lifeboat which served at Southend-on-Sea and Beaumaris, was typical of the design of lifeboat operated by the RNLI during the first half of the 20th century. Built of wood with a top speed of 9 knots, the Watson and Barnett designs were not self-righting when built. At the time of the introduction of the 44ft lifeboat to Britain, these types formed the backbone of the RNLI's fleet.
(From a postcard in the author's collection)

37ft Oakley *Jane Hay (ON.974)* on trials off Littlehampton prior to entering service at St Abbs, in the Scottish Borders. The Oakley design, when introduced into service in 1958, was seen as a major advance in lifeboat design. Not only did it have good seakeeping abilities but it was also self-righting, a combination never achieved before in a British lifeboat design. However, the hull shape restricted its speed to around 9 knots. (RNLI)

The RNLI's interest in the USCG 44ft lifeboat was a significant development, particularly when seen in the context of post-1945 lifeboat development in the UK. During World War II the lifeboat service had operated under difficult conditions as lifeboats were forced to work under the guidance of the naval authorities. Moreover, with the country's economy focused entirely on the war effort, fund-raising for charitable causes had been exceptionally difficult. Few new lifeboats had been built and so once peace had been secured the RNLI embarked upon a rapid construction programme. In 1945, the fleet consisted of 151 motor and three pulling lifeboats. The first priority for the Institution, therefore, was to equip all stations with motor lifeboats.

Between 1945 and 1960, over 100 new motor lifeboats were constructed, an average of eight per annum. However, these new boats, of the Watson, Barnett and Liverpool types, were based on a 19th century hull design, albeit with improved equipment, more powerful engines and twin screws. This hull design, which typified British lifeboats up to the 1960s, was introduced in the 1890s in a then radical design of sailing lifeboat. Drawn up by George Lennox Watson, the RNLI's Naval Architect, it remained the predominant hull shape for non-self-righting lifeboats until the introduction of the USCG's 44ft design.

Some improvements had been implemented in the immediate post-war years. Developments included the introduction of a midship-steering position in the 46ft 9in Watson class of motor lifeboat. In addition, a policy of fitting all lifeboats with diesel engines was pursued. But the RNLI believed at this time that new and relatively untried ideas and equipment should not be introduced into the lifeboat service. In 1947, the RNLI's Chief inspector of Lifeboats, Commander P. E. Vaux, stated that "a lifeboat is not the medium to experiment with", and added that every part of a lifeboat should be "thoroughly tested and proved to the hilt." Significant advances were thus not implemented by the RNLI and the latest technology not employed, and although some design changes were made, nothing radical was introduced.

Although boats based on the design were fine, seaworthy craft, well-suited to rescue work during the first half of the 20th century, they had two major drawbacks. Firstly, they were not self-righting and, secondly, the hull shape restricted speed to, at best, a little over 9 knots irrespective of engine size and power. The first significant advance of the post-War era came during the late 1950s with the introduction of a 37ft lifeboat which overcame the problem of self-righting and was hailed as a major breakthrough. Designed by Richard Oakley, after whom it was subsequently named, the new design was both inherently stable and also self-righting, a combination that had eluded lifeboat designers until then.

Self-righting boats had sacrificed some of their initial stability to achieve self-righting, and this meant they were not popular with crews around the coast. Oakley's new design, however, was both self-righting by virtue of a water-ballast transfer tank, and its hull shape, similar to that in the Watson and Barnett non-self-righting lifeboats, provided great stability. But the displacement hull meant speed was limited. This type of hull has to push water out of the way as it moves, creating drag and making it almost impossible to achieve a speed greater than 9 knots. At the time of the introduction of the new lifeboat, a faster design was needed.

International Lifeboat Conference 1963

The next major breakthrough in lifeboat development in Britain came after the RNLI hosted the International Lifeboat Conference in Edinburgh between 4 and 6 June 1963. The aim of the International Conferences, held every four years, is to exchange rescue ideas to mutually benefit lifeboat organisations around the world. At Edinburgh, 35 papers on a variety of subjects connected with lifeboats and life-saving were read and discussed. The RNLI presented papers on first aid in lifeboats, the building of new lifeboat stations at Selsey and Lizard and the prototype 48ft 6in Oakley type lifeboat. Delegates from Norway, Sweden, Netherlands and the United States gave papers on newly developed lifeboat designs built in their countries.

The 44ft design described by the USCG delegation, primarily intended for general purpose inshore rescue work off the American coasts, was of particular interest to several lifeboat institutions, including the RNLI. The USCG explained that the boat was the product of the most comprehensive design, construction and evaluation project ever undertaken for a Coast Guard rescue craft. Lieutenant Commander Witter, of the USCG's Naval Engineering Division, prefaced his description of the design by saying:

RNLI prototype 44-001, ex-USCG CG-44328, seen on 13 April 1964 at the US Coast Guard yard, Curtis Bay, shortly after building work had been completed. (Official USCG photo, from the collection of William Wilkinson)

Seen from the port quarter, 44-001 has both US and British ensigns hoisted, symbolising the close cooperation between both countries to design and develop improved lifeboat types. (Official USCG photo, from the collection of William Wilkinson)

"The CG-44300 [the prototype] . . . is considered by this command to be the most remarkable piece of equipment to bolster the operational capabilities of the Coast Guard since the development of the 52-foot MLB."

With such praise it is hardly surprising that considerable interest was shown by other delegations at the Conference. Although it was not possible to bring one of the new 44-footers to the Conference, a film of the boat in action manoeuvring through the extreme surf conditions regularly encountered on the Pacific coast was shown. A model was also presented for the delegates to examine. Commander de Booy, Director of the KNZHRM (North and South Netherlands Lifeboat Society), was very impressed with the boat and said "If you could spare one of these 44ft boats we would like to try her on our coast."

The discussion at the Conference covered various areas of the new boat's design and operation. Witter explained that all 44-footers were kept afloat as the USCG was phasing out launch-ways and boathouses because they were so costly to maintain. He also stated that fitting radar in the steering position was not yet practicable because the unit must be watertight and such a unit had yet to be found. The question of rudder protection was also raised, but in Witter's view the rudders were well enough protected. He described an incident in which one of the boats was stranded accidentally and driven on to the beach. She was driven off under her own power, and driven back to sea again on the next surf surge having suffered minimal damage.

Acquisition by the RNLI of the 44-footer

The RNLI's Conference Delegation, led by the Right Honourable the Earl Howe, was very impressed by the new USCG design and realised that the 44ft motor lifeboat could meet the institution's initial requirements for a faster rescue boat. After careful consideration by the Institution's boat and construction committee, the Committee of Management decided in 1963 that a delegation should be sent to examine the USCG lifeboat and one should be acquired for trials. Designing a 'fast afloat boat' from scratch was unnecessary when it became apparent to the RNLI that such a craft was already designed. Not only had it been built, but it had also been tested in extreme conditions on the American seaboard.

In January 1964 a small delegation from the Institution, led by the chairman Captain the Hon V. M. Wyndham-Quin, visited the United States to inspect USCG craft and in particular the 44ft steel lifeboat. The delegation consisted of Commander F. R. H. Swann, chairman of the boat and construction committee, Peter Guinness and N Warrington Smyth, both members of the boat and construction committee, and Lieut-Commander W. L. Gerard Dutton, Chief Inspector of lifeboats.

After preliminary discussions in Washington, the delegation visited the Coast Guard yard at Curtis Bay, Baltimore, Maryland, and saw a number of the 44ft steel-hulled boats under construction. They also saw other CG craft in action, including an 82ft cutter and amphibious

After being used for trials and evaluation, 44-001 was placed in the RNLI's Relief Fleet, and she served throughout her career at stations whose lifeboat was away for refit or overhaul. This fine photograph shows her leaving Gorleston harbour on 9 November 1975 for the annual Remembrance Service. (Eastern Counties Newspapers, courtesy of Paul Russell)

The seventh Waveney to be built by the RNLI, ON.1026, allocated to Eyemouth, under construction at Groves & Guttridge yard, Cowes, IOW, in July 1972. (Jeff Morris)

Outside Brooke Marine, Lowestoft, on 31 August 1967, *Margaret Graham* (44-005), the fourth Waveney to be built for the RNLI, seen prior to going to Harwich. (Jeff Morris)

aircraft and helicopters. An exercise was arranged for the delegation's benefit in which a 44ft motor lifeboat took the 1300-ton *Sassafras* in tow. Using a nylon line the lifeboat maintained a speed of nearly six knots. Not only were the 44ft lifeboats fully self-righting and excellent sea boats, but they also had very good towing capabilities.

On returning to London the delegation reported to the Committee of Management, who decided to acquire one of the 44ft vessels for evaluation purposes. The USCG Commandant agreed to make a fully-equipped boat available for evaluation and service in the United Kingdom under the colours of the RNLI. The 28th boat off the Curtis Bay production line was allocated to the RNLI. After successful sea trials in America with the RNLI's Chief Inspector, Lieut-Commander Dutton, on board, the boat was accepted by the RNLI and shipped from Baltimore to the United Kingdom as deck cargo on a vessel.

The boat arrived in London in May 1964 and became the prototype vessel, numbered 44-001 by the RNLI. She then commenced extensive trials round the coasts of Great Britain and the Republic of Ireland. In December 1964, trials were carried out off the Dutch coast in association with the Royal

South Holland Lifeboat Society (KZHMRS), which expressed interest in the boat at the 1963 Conference. The boat was then submitted to trials by a large number of crews and used to train them to handle such boats. The last stages of her trials were carried out off the coasts of Scotland and north-east England, after which she was taken south. The initial evaluation period lasted until September 1965, during which nearly 5000 miles were covered by the boat.

Construction of the 44-footers in Britain

At the time of the trials of the USCG design, no RNLI lifeboat was capable of a speed greater than 9 knots. The speed of the new 44ft lifeboat was achieved by the hull design, which was of a semi-planing form. The traditional British lifeboat designs were based around a displacement double-ended hull form. Semi-planing hulls lift out of the water when a certain speed is reached, reducing the amount of drag and thus enabling a greater speed to be achieved. The 44-footer's hull shape was therefore a radical departure from previous British lifeboat designs.

Although completely different from any lifeboat in Britain, and thus initially something of a curiosity to lifeboat crews,

British prototype technical details

Details of the USCG steel lifeboat comparing the original to the first British-built boat.

	A. 44-001 *US prototype supplied to RNLI*	B. 44-002 *First British-built Waveney*
Length, overall	44'10½"	44'10½"
Length, design waterline	40'	40'
Beam, overall	12'8"	12'8"
Beam, waterline	10'10"	10'10"
Draft	3'2½"	3'11"
Displacement	15.8 tons	17 tons
Fuel capacity	333 US gallons	350 gallons
Water capacity	16 US gallons	15 gallons
Shaft horsepower, maximum	400	400 (one hour rating)
Speed	15.3 knots	14 knots
Endurance	290m at 10 knots, 163m at 15 knots	205m at 12 knots, 305m at 10 knots
Range of stability	In excess of 175 degrees	180 degrees

SOURCES: A. *The Lifeboat*, Vol.38, June 1964, p.67
B. International Lifeboat Conference *Report*, 1967, Item No.3, p.24

the extended trials of 44-001 were an unqualified success. The boat proved capable of operating in all conditions encountered in the UK and Ireland so the RNLI decided to build six further boats to the design. From the documents put at the RNLI's disposal by the USCG, specifications and comprehensive drawings were prepared. Changes were made to British material specifications where possible, and from American to British components and equipment. With the exception of the main engines and a small number of minor items, British equipment was specified in order to facilitate construction in Britain.

The RNLI's specifications also incorporated a number of changes to the US design. These included an additional fuel tank, the construction of a double bottom beneath the

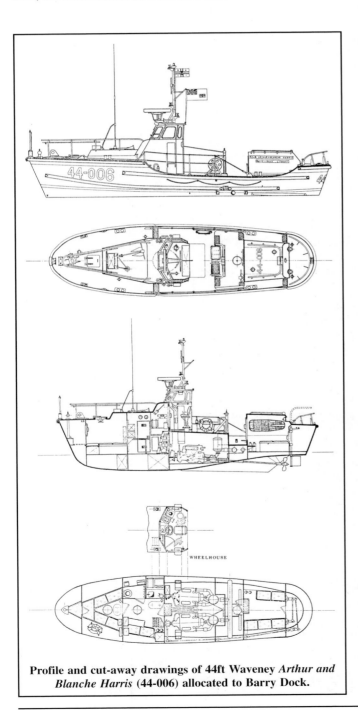

Profile and cut-away drawings of 44ft Waveney *Arthur and Blanche Harris* (44-006) allocated to Barry Dock.

Alterations and additions by the RNLI

1. Aluminium alloy main deck, in place of steel.
2. After cabin increased in height by 2 inches and coachroof forward of steering shelter increased in volume to improve self-righting ability.
3. Increased weather protection for helmsman by fitting permanent sides and windows to the open wheelhouse, in place of portable screens.
4. Bolted "A" brackets in place of welded "P" brackets.
5. Electric windlass fitted, in place of hand anchor recovery.
6. Two 65lb anchors fitted, in place of one 60lb and one 30lb.
7. Pushpit rails fitted to raised deck aft.
8. Mathway mechanical steering gear fitted, in place of hydraulic gear.
9. Foam-filled double-bottom fitted in engine room. Foam also filled in forepeak, port and starboard at after end of crews cabin and in centre section of the void space below the well deck.
10. Reserve fuel tank fitted between frame 4 and 5.
11. Engine room ventilators draw air from inside the steering position, to prevent spray from entering the engine room.
12. Wave subduing system fitted.
13. Battery boxes recessed into tank top in crew's cabin.
14. Windscreen washing system fitted.
15. Port and starboard navigation lights fitted in screens on wheelhouse top.
16. Natural ventilation system fitted to after cabin with RNLI design inlet and outlet valves.
17. Toilet compartment removed, and this space fitted out as radio operator's area.
18. RNLI duplex scuppers fitted in both wells in addition to the ball valves.
19. Ford Mermaid engines of 250bhp installed, in place of Cummins 215bhp.
20. Better diesel generator fitted for battery charging.
21. Two fire hydrants and two fire and bilge pumps driven by main engines, in place of one hydrant and one pump with one engine room bilge eductor.
22. Fixed bilge suctions fitted in engine room.
23. Water injected stern exhausts, in place of transverse exhausts.
24. Electrical distribution by double pole circuit breakers.
25. Engine room fire extinguishing system operated from the wheelhouse.
26. D/F and Decca Navigator installed.
27. Intercom system with master unit in wheelhouse serving after cabin, crew's cabin, forward cabin and fore deck.
28. Depth recorder fitted in crew's cabin in addition to indicator in wheelhouse.
29. Transmission and reception of M/F radio from wheelhouse in addition to radio operator's position.
30. Single whip aerial on the forward casing replaced by two whip aerials on wheelhouse front.

The first RNLI 44ft Waveney, *John F Kennedy* (44-002), was also the first steel-hulled lifeboat to enter service in the British Isles. (RNLI)

The second Waveney to be built by the RNLI, *Khami* (44-003), being lifted out of the water at Gorleston for her annual hull inspection on 13 September 1977. This excellent photograph clearly shows the propeller and rudder arrangement on the Waveneys. One of the fins fitted to the side of the hull, to improve the trim of the boat, can also be seen. (Eastern Counties Newspapers, courtesy of Paul Russell)

The third Waveney built for the RNLI, *Faithful Forester* (44-004), completed in 1967 and stationed at Dover. This photograph shows her with a white superstructure on exercise in the English Channel. (John G Callis)

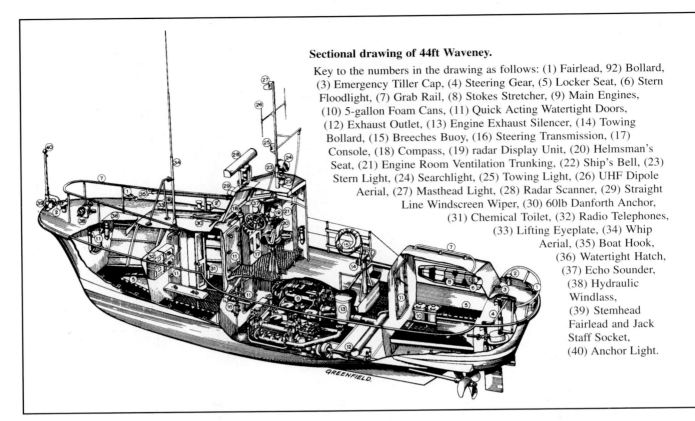

Sectional drawing of 44ft Waveney.

Key to the numbers in the drawing as follows: (1) Fairlead, 92) Bollard, (3) Emergency Tiller Cap, (4) Steering Gear, (5) Locker Seat, (6) Stern Floodlight, (7) Grab Rail, (8) Stokes Stretcher, (9) Main Engines, (10) 5-gallon Foam Cans, (11) Quick Acting Watertight Doors, (12) Exhaust Outlet, (13) Engine Exhaust Silencer, (14) Towing Bollard, (15) Breeches Buoy, (16) Steering Transmission, (17) Console, (18) Compass, (19) radar Display Unit, (20) Helmsman's Seat, (21) Engine Room Ventilation Trunking, (22) Ship's Bell, (23) Stern Light, (24) Searchlight, (25) Towing Light, (26) UHF Dipole Aerial, (27) Masthead Light, (28) Radar Scanner, (29) Straight Line Windscreen Wiper, (30) 60lb Danforth Anchor, (31) Chemical Toilet, (32) Radio Telephones, (33) Lifting Eyeplate, (34) Whip Aerial, (35) Boat Hook, (36) Watertight Hatch, (37) Echo Sounder, (38) Hydraulic Windlass, (39) Stemhead Fairlead and Jack Staff Socket, (40) Anchor Light.

machinery compartment, an extended wheelhouse to improve crew protection, raised fore and after cabin tops to improve the self-righting ability, and an additional power take-off on the starboard engine to drive a hydraulic pump unit for the operation of a windlass.

The hull was constructed from Corten steel because it was decided at the outset that the vessel should be kept as near as possible to the original design of the USCG. Corten was supposed to have greater resistance to corrosion than any other steel. However, the main deck plating and wheelhouse were constructed of aluminium alloy, rather than steel as on the USCG version. These modifications were not carried out retrospectively on 44-001, which therefore remained different from the British-built boats.

In the Summer of 1965 tenders were invited for building six boats of the new design. The contract was awarded to the Lowestoft firm of Brooke Marine Ltd, which began construction towards the end of 1965. The first boat was completed 36 weeks after the RNLI had placed the order, while the total cost of the new boats was approximately £158,700. As the boatyard which built the first six boats was situated on the river Waveney, the type was given the class name "Waveney" and it has been RNLI policy ever since to name lifeboat classes after rivers.

The first seven Waveneys (including 44-001) were built with Cummins main engines, model V6N215M, fitted with a reverse and 3:1 reduction gearbox, type 76/100, made by the then Parsons Engineering Co Ltd, of Southampton, giving a speed of 13 knots. The next seven boats (44-008 to 44-015) were built with General Motors diesels, and the remainder had either Ford Mermaid or Caterpillar diesels, which gave a maximum speed of 16 knots. The earlier boats were subsequently re-engined with Caterpillar diesels. 44-001

steamed in excess of 5000 hours on her original Cummins type V200 engines. During 1974 she was re-engined with Ford Mermaid 595 turbo-plus units developing 250bhp each, which gave her a speed of 16 knots.

A variety of electronic equipment was installed, different from that in the US boats, and upgraded as improved models became available. Initially, the electronic equipment comprised a Kelvin Hughes Type 17 radar, with watertight pattern display unit in the wheelhouse; Redifon UHF and VHF/MF radio telephone; Woodsons type 90 MF radio equipment; and a Ferrograph combined echo sounder unit. The deckheads and sides of the boat throughout the accommodation were lined with plastic foam heat and sound insulation. All exterior steelwork and some interior steelwork was shot blasted prior to painting.

The designated number of crew on the Waveney was five, but often six or seven crew members would be taken on service. The design provided relatively good crew protection, although the Coxswain was seated in an open wheelhouse that offered only limited shelter. Seats were provided for the crew in the cabin, but it was usual for them to remain on deck behind the wheelhouse. The crew's cabin was fitted with a settee seat, limited galley facilities, and a toilet. There were two cabins, fore and aft, which provided seating for survivors, and a stretcher stowed in the aft cabin.

The first RNLI-built 44ft Waveney to enter service was *John F Kennedy,* which was placed on station at Dun Laoghaire, to cover the waters of Dublin Bay and the Irish Sea, in May 1967. Although some of the RNLI's crews were initially disconcerted by the relatively low stability of the design, caused by the hull shape and the need for self-righting, the general behaviour and high power of the boats, which enabled them to pull clear of any dangerous situation, soon endeared them to lifeboatmen all round the coast.

The success with which the 44ft design had been adapted for use in Britain demonstrated to other sea rescue organisations the possibilities it offered. Well suited to a wide variety of sea conditions, the 44ft design has been used extensively throughout the world. While the RNLI were beginning their Waveney building programme, interest was being shown by the USCG's neighbours in Canada and in 1966 the Canadian Government bought one for use by the Canadian Coast Guard (CCG). On 14 September that year the 44-footer was loaded on board the ice-breaking ship *Edward Cornwallis* and taken to Canada. Since then, the CCG have used 44-footers on both East and West coasts. They operated with a red hull, but the livery altered between a white superstructure and SAR yellow. All the Canadian 44-footers had enclosed wheelhouses, which some crew found to be very claustrophobic. However, as in Britain and the United States, they served with distinction.

In Europe, organisations in Norway, Portugal and Italy have all used the 44ft design. In 1968, two 44ft boats entered service with the Norwegian Society for the Rescue of the Shipwrecked. R/S 73 and R/S 74, named *Ole O Hoshovde* and *Arne Fahlstrøm* respectively, were operated in Norway until the mid-1970s. The boats were altered by enclosing the wheelhouse for improved operation in the extreme cold experienced in Norwegian waters. The 44ft design was also used by the Italian Coast Guard and by the lifeboat service in Portugal, which had two constructed. Both were built by the Navy Shipyard in Portugal, the first completed in 1978 was named *Sota-Patrão António Crista* and the second, completed in 1979, named *Patrão Joaquim Casaca*. In 1975, ten boats were built for the Imperial Iranian Navy by Fairey Marine at Cowes, under license from the US Government. The Iranian Navy paid $56,400 to the USCG but it is not known how the boats were used in Iran.

44ft lifeboats operated at the limits

The strength and sturdiness of the 44ft lifeboat is perhaps best illustrated by the following statistics about CG-44300: by

44ft Motor Lifeboats operated by the Canadian Coastguard

No.	Year	Builder	Designation
CG 101	1966	USCG Shipyard, Curtis Bay, Maryland	Clarks Harbour/ Westmount
CG 102	1969	Chantier Maritimes du St Laurent, Paspédiac	Westport
CG 103	1969	Chantier Maritimes du St Laurent, Paspédiac	Bickerton/ Jan.1994- Kestrel
CG 104	1969	McKay Cormack Ltd, Victoria, BC	Bamfield
CG 105	1970	McKay Cormack Ltd, Victoria, BC	Tofino
CG 106	1970	McKay Cormack Ltd, Victoria, BC	Bull Harbour/ Port Hardy
CG 107	1973	Georgetown Shipyard, Georgetown, PEI	Burin
CG 108	1973	Georgetown Shipyard, Georgetown, PEI	Twilingate/ 1978-9 Tobermory
CG 109	1973	Georgetown Shipyard, Georgetown, PEI	St-Anthony/ Thunder Bay/ 1978-9 Westfort
CG 114	1973	Georgetown Shipyard, Georgetown, PEI	Burgeo
CG 115	1975	Eastern Equipment, Montréal, Que	Shippagan
CG 116	1975	Eastern Equipment, Montréal, Que	Clark's Harbour
CG 117	1975	Eastern Equipment, Montréal, Que	Sambro
CG 118	1975	Eastern Equipment, Montréal, Que	Louisbourg
CG 140	1982	Georgetown Shipyard, Georgetown, PEI	Port Mouton
CG 141	1982	Georgetown Shipyard, Georgetown, PEI	Cap-aux-Meules
	1985	Hike Metal Products, Wheatley, Ont	Cap Goélands
	1985	Hike Metal Products, Wheatley, Ont	Souris/ Westmount (training)

One of the two 44-footers built for service in Portugal, *Patrao Joaquim Casaca*, was virtually identical to Waveneys built by the RNLI. (From a photo in the author's collection)

A Canadian Coastguard 44-footer seen on exercise. The CCG modified the design to fully enclose the wheelhouse, and this is clearly visible in this photo. (Clay Evans)

Above **Operating in the ice, CG-44389 shows the strength of the 44-footer's steel hull. (Supplied by Clive Lawford)**

Below **Chincoteague 44ft motor lifeboat CG-44367 moored at her station, showing the nylon dodger foul weather curtain at the rear of the wheelhouse. (Supplied by Clive Lawford)**

A fine photograph of USCG 44ft motor lifeboat CG-44392, clearly showing the design's raked bow. (Official USCG photo)

1995, this boat had capsized six times, gone end-over-end three times and once been rammed by a freighter. Yet it was still afloat and had kept its crews alive proving that the 44-footer was able to cope in the most extreme circumstances. The ability to self-right, a requirement of the original design, was clearly an essential feature particularly for operations in the heavy surf typical of America's western seaboard. The enormous breaking waves at the river bars are often over 20ft in height, and make the possibility of capsizing high. Indeed, the self-righting abilities of the design were put to the test soon after it entered service. Within its first five years of service, three were capsized, and all righted without loss of life.

One of these capsizes occurred on 11 June 1966 on the Umpqua River Bar, Oregon. On that day, CG-44303 was on patrol with CG-36514 standing by craft coming into the river through breaking swells 25ft in height, some larger. While guarding the danger areas, a large series of swells began moving in, picking up height as they approached CG-44303. CG-44303 was in a trough and headed straight in line with the swell, but her bow was digging into the back of the swell ahead. As the swell astern broke, the stern of CG-44303 was caught in the curl of the wave and the boat was turned over. The Coxswain, Thomas Adams, shouted "hang on" to the other crew members and then all were submerged.

The boat settled in the overturned position and then slowly righted itself. The Coxswain was strapped into his seat and remained there; another crew member was thrown against the preventer screen at the rear of the wheelhouse; and the third crew member was carried away by the water, but was soon picked up once the boat had righted. Both engines were still running, in neutral, and after the third crew member had been picked out of heavy swell the boat was taken into calm water where the crew examined her.

During the capsize, approximately 700 to 1000 gallons of water had been sucked into the engine room through the air breather vents and oil had spilled from the hydraulic starting motor reservoir. Apart from this, much of the gear had survived; most damage occurred on the top side of the vessel. Everything above the deckhouse had been carried away completely or bent. The main mast and radar dome antenna were gone, the fire hose had been thrown over the bow and the aluminium rod holding the hose in place torn off. In his report of the incident, Coxswain Adams noted that while the 44-footer performs extremely competently in rough seas, being caught in the curl of a large breaker is the most dangerous position to be in, although in this instance the boat's inherent structural resilience ensured its survival with only minimal damage to the equipment.

As a result of this capsize, a study of the behaviour of equipment on board CG-44303 was undertaken by USCG design teams. They subsequently recommended a number of minor changes be made to the 44-footer's design. CG-44303 was delayed in righting when its superstructure struck the bottom. Tests on the righting behaviour of the design showed that the boat would not right when capsized unless external forces roll it 40 degrees from the capsized vertical. To improve the righting capabilities of the boat, it was therefore recommended that the centre of buoyancy be raised, the centre of gravity lowered and buoyant foam placed on the underside of the wheelhouse where ample headroom was available. With regard to engine room flooding, which would

A USCG 44-footer crossing one of the bars common on the American seaboard. The 44-footers were regularly called upon to cross such bars, where extreme surf conditions were usually encountered. (Official USCG photo)

The prototype USCG 44-footer CG-44300 covered by surf on the rugged bar at the entrance to Newport Harbor, Oregon, operated by a crew of three from Yaquina Bay Lifeboat Station. The ability to operate in heavy breaking surf, as illustrated here, was one of the factors the designers of the 44-footer had to take into account. (Official USCG photo)

also have a detrimental effect on the boat's righting ability, an automatic shut-off was fitted so that, if the boat was in the capsized position, the engines would not continue to run and suck water through the air intake ducts.

Since the first checks on the boat's self-righting capability were made in 1967, periodic checks have taken place to monitor the stability of the boats. In 1967 it was decided that although the boat was stable in the capsized position, the effort necessary to bring the boat upright was so small that alterations were unnecessary. Further tests were made in May 1971 when CG-44396 was capsized under controlled conditions at the Coast Guard Yard. The righting ability of the boat had improved since 1967 as a result of weight reduction achieved through the removal

of both hydraulic starting systems and lower rubber fenders.

The design's self-righting ability was again put to the test for real on 26 November 1973. CG-44373 rolled over four times in heavy surf at Gleneden Beach, Oregon. All four crew members, having been thrown off the boat, were rescued from the water by helicopter. The most serious injury any of them sustained was a fractured shoulder blade. The boat lost its windshield structure, all exterior electronics, and the forward and after cabin tops, as well as the engine vents, were partially crushed. However, the engines were still running when the boat was washed up on the beach and only about 300 gallons of water had entered the engine room. The boat grounded in the upright position and this, together with the fact that the engines were still running, was testament to the seaworthiness of the boat, the excellence of the original design, its strong construction and the high standards of maintenance.

Further capsizes of USCG 44ft motor lifeboats have occurred. In 1975, one capsized in Alaska and although the crew were rescued, the boat itself was lost. Sadly, the crew of one of the two 44ft motor lifeboats from the Quillayute River Station were not so fortunate during a capsize in February 1997. When their boat turned over, three out of the four Coast Guard crewmen on board were lost: Seaman Clinton Miniken, Petty Officer 2nd Class David Bosley and Petty Officer 3rd Class Matthew Schlimme. Nineteen-year-old Seaman Apprentice Benjamin Wingo, the most junior member

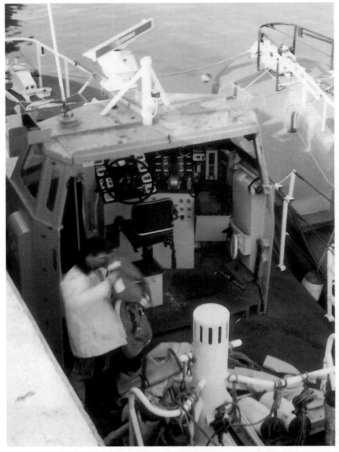

of the team, survived. This was the first capsizing of a 44-footer in 35 years of service with the USCG in which crews' lives had been lost.

The capsized boat was one of two sent out from the Quillayute River Station, along with a helicopter, to assist two people on a sailboat who radioed that they were taking on water in heavy seas near the Olympic Peninsula town of La Push. The boat got caught parallel to incoming waves and, in the trough of two waves, capsized three times and was washed up deep inside a cove on James Island, just off the coast. Each time it capsized, it righted as designed but the crew members were washed overboard. District Commander for the Pacific Northwest, Coast Guard Admiral J. David Spade, said "It's the worst tragedy I have ever experienced in my command." The sailboat's passengers were rescued by the helicopter.

Although several 44-footers have capsized during service with the USCG, only once in Britain has a 44ft Waveney capsized on service. When built in Britain, aluminium rather than steel was used for deck and wheelhouse. This reduced weight above the waterline which in turn lowered the centre of gravity and improved the righting ability by making the boat less stable in the inverted position. This righting ability was put to the test on 28 February 1993 when the Waveney operating from Hartlepool, *The Scout*, was twice capsized on service to the tanker *Freja Svea* in severe conditions off the north-east coast.

The lifeboat was standing by the tanker when, climbing at an angle up a 30ft to 40ft sea, she was laid over hard to port as she neared the wave's curling crest. With no water on the other side, she fell into the trough of the wave and capsized. The lifeboat performed exactly as she was designed to and righted. None of the crew on board were lost, though some sustained minor injuries. One crew member was washed overboard but was safely picked up by an RAF helicopter. The lifeboat was damaged by the force of the water and escorted back to station by the lifeboat from the neighbouring Teesmouth station. Only minor structural damage was sustained, caused mainly by water pressure. The mast sheered, the searchlight was bent over and the after cabin had some indentations. Bolts holding down the Coxswain's seat were sheered when a crew member was thrown through the air and hit the seat.

Capsizes are, fortunately, few and far between. More noteworthy are the many rescues which the 44-footers have performed in the US; most were routine, but some were remarkable as the courage and stamina of Coast Guardsmen

Upper **The damage to Hartlepool's Waveney *The Scout* (44-018) suffered during the capsizes in February 1993 was mainly to the craft's aerials and mast mounted on the wheelhouse, as can be seen in this photograph. (Photo supplied by R W Williams)**

Lower **The forward rope storage box of *The Scout* (44-018) bent by the force of water during the capsizes. (Photo supplied by R W Williams)**

was demonstrated, as was the outstanding capabilities of the lifeboat. On 1 August 1985, the 44-footer from Gloucester Station, Massachusetts, set out at 7.30am in heavy weather to the assistance of the disabled fishing vessel *Global Cape Ann*. Stranded near Wild Cat Knoll, about 35 miles east of Gloucester, it took the lifeboat four hours to reach the casualty, battling through winds gusting to 40 knots and waves reaching 18ft in height.

The lifeboat took the fishing vessel in tow and set a course for Gloucester. The two craft were heading into the wind and waves, making only 3 knots. At this speed, it would have taken 10 hours to reach Gloucester, so the crew of the 44-footer took turns on the helm to reduce fatigue. After about 3 hours the weather improved so speed was increased to 6 knots. It was 8.45pm when the vessels finally reached port and moored alongside having battled through some of the worst conditions experienced by those on board.

In Britain, Waveneys have also performed outstanding rescues in extreme conditions. One of the most difficult rescues took place in 1987 when the crew of the Waveney at Sheerness, *Helen Turnbull* (ON.1027), encountered high winds and heavy seas. On 16 October that year much of southern England was struck by a full hurricane, which caused severe damage both on land and at sea. At about 6am *Helen Turnbull* put out after red flares had been sighted. As the lifeboat headed out to sea, winds in excess of 90 knots were being recorded. At one point she was hit by an extremely heavy, breaking sea which swung her round until she was beam on to the waves. The Coxswain, Robin Castle, through skilful use of the engines, was able to bring the lifeboat round again and back on course.

In waves up to 25ft high the lifeboat was pitching and rolling violently, while visibility was reduced to almost zero due to flying spray and frequent heavy rain squalls. At 7.17am the casualty, a 16ft cabin cruiser, was spotted by one of the lifeboatmen. The cruiser was slowly sinking as huge waves crashed over her. Despite the shallow water in which the casualty was stranded, Coxswain Castle took the lifeboat

A routine service for 44-001 while on relief duty at Newhaven, bringing in the disabled trawler *George Clements* on 24 October 1981. (Jeff Morris)

Entering Troon harbour, *Connel Elizabeth Cargill* (44-007) brings in the disabled tug *Garnock* which had a damaged propeller and steering gear. (Ian Johnson)

At the entrance to Whitby harbour, *The White Rose of Yorkshire* (44-012) escorts in the local keelboat *Radiant Morn* in October 1985. The Waveney was ideal for operating in the heavy breaking surf often encountered at Whitby harbour entrance. She was frequently called upon to assist local fishing craft entering the harbour, as in this instance. (Paul Arro)

Involved in several dramatic and medal-winning rescues, *Helen Turnball* (44-009) is seen here during a routine exercise off Sheerness Docks. (Nicholas Leach)

Khami (44-003) leading *Barham* (44-021) into Gorleston harbour on 29 May 1980, escorted by the station's Atlantic 21 *Waveney Forester* (B-530). At both Gorleston and Harwich new Waveneys were built to replace older ones. (Eastern Daily Press, courtesy of Paul Russell)

alongside and the two men on board were quickly hauled onto the lifeboat. As the lifeboat came astern to clear the cruiser, a gust of wind swung the lifeboat around, her stern ran aground and despite strenuous efforts on the part of the lifeboatmen she remained fast aground.

After assessing the situation, the engines were shut down and the lifeboatmen, except the Coxswain and Second Coxswain, went below deck and the watertight doors were closed. The VHF radio was left on to maintain contact with the shore. When the water receded, the lifeboatmen examined the lifeboat's hull to ensure no damage had been sustained. Both propellers and rudders were clear and at 6.17pm with the water rising the lifeboat floated clear. Using the spare anchor she was pulled off the sands and returned to Sheerness Docks at 7.15pm, by when the wind had dropped to force 6.

For this service, the Bronze Medal for Gallantry was awarded by the RNLI to Coxswain Castle for his

demonstration of truly outstanding seamanship. The Thanks of the Institution inscribed on Vellum was accorded to Second Coxswain Dennis Bailey and lifeboatman Richard Rogers, while Medal Service Certificates were presented to each of the other crewmembers, Peter Bullin, Eamon Finch and Brian Spoor. This service was carried out in the most extreme conditions and again proved the 44ft Waveney to be of exceptional design and construction. The boat's sturdiness and power had enabled two lives to be saved while the boat itself had sustained no damage.

Leaving service

The twenty-second and last Waveney built by the RNLI, *The William and Jane* (ON.1079) was completed in 1982 and went on station at Blyth in October of that year. She entered service two decades after the design was first introduced in the United States. Although an outstanding design, as technology and naval architecture advanced, by the 1990s

Summary of Medal-winning rescues in Britain

Silver Medal rescues

1.12.1975	Dover	*Faithful Forester*	Coxswain Arthur Liddon
23.7.1980	Sheerness	*Helen Turnbull*	Coxswain/Mechanic Charles Bowry
12.9.1980	Troon	*Connel Elizabeth Cargill*	Coxswain/Mechanic Ian Johnson
3.9.1983	St Helier	*Thomas James King*	Coxswain Michael Berry
26.12.1986	Ramsgate	*Ralph and Joy Swann*	Coxswain/Mechanic Ron Cannon
6.10.1990	Eyemouth	44-001 (relief)	Acting Coxswain James Dougal

Bronze Medal rescues

15.1.1970	Gorleston	*Khami*	Coxswain John Bryan
13.12.1974	Gorleston	*Khami*	Coxswain John Bryan
16.8.1975	Sheerness	*Helen Turnbull*	Coxswain/Mech Charles Bowry
1.12.1975	Dover	*Faithful Forester*	2nd Coxswain Anthony Hawkins
9.7.1976	Dunmore East	*St Patrick*	Coxswain/Mech Stephen Whittle
15.2.1978	Plymouth	*Thomas Forehead and Mary Rowse II*	Acting Coxswain Patrick Marshall
15.2.1978	Plymouth	*Thomas Forehead and Mary Rowse II*	Mechanic Cyril Alcock
30.12.1978	Sheerness	*Helen Turnbull*	Coxswain/Mech Charles Bowry
22.12.1979	Gorleston	*Khami*	Coxswain/Mech Richard Hawkins
7.12.1982	Blyth	*The William and Jane*	Coxswain Charles Hatcher
14.12.1982	St Helier	*Faithful Forester* (relief)	Coxswain Michael Berry
10.11.1985	Hartlepool	*The Scout*	Coxswain Robert Maiden
16.10.1987	Sheerness	*Helen Turnbull*	Coxswain/Mech Robin Castle
9.4.1988	Whitby	*The White Rose of Yorkshire*	Coxswain/Mech Peter Thomson

One of the early 44ft lifeboats built by the RNLI, *Khami* (44-003) was stationed at Great Yarmouth and Gorleston in August 1967. She proved her worth on the East Coast, saving 71 lives and being used in three medal-winning services. (Eastern Daily Press)

14m Trent *Roy Barker I* (ON.1199) at Alderney in April 2000. The Trent, introduced into service in 1994, replaced the Waveney and incorporated better crew protection as well as greater speed, capable of reaching 25 knots. (Nicholas Leach)

The prototype USCG 47ft motor lifeboat CG-44200 on trials off Victoria, Canada. Although the second prototype, CG-47201 was painted in a white colour scheme, most 47-footers were not painted but left in their natural silver/grey aluminium colour, as in this photo, to reduce maintenance costs. (Clay Evans)

more sophisticated boats were being developed and plans for its replacement were underway on both sides of the Atlantic. While the level of crew protection was praised when the design was first introduced, by this time a fully enclosed wheelhouse, providing complete crew protection, was seen as an essential feature while even greater speed was sought.

With the introduction of two new classes of all-weather lifeboat, the 17m Severn and 14m Trent, in 1994, the Waveneys were phased out of service. Both new designs had fully enclosed, heated wheelhouses, and could achieve speeds up to 25 knots, almost twice that of the Waveney. At the majority of stations, the Waveney was replaced by a Trent, although at some stations the larger Severn was deployed in its place. Following withdrawal from station, the RNLI placed the boats on their sale list. The first Waveney to be withdrawn from service was 44-002, *John F Kennedy*

(ON.1001), and she was sold out of service in August 1996. In Ireland, where *John F Kennedy,* the RNLI's first Waveney, had been stationed, the last Waveney to leave was *The William and Jane,* from Larne, in November 1998.

The last Waveney in the RNLI fleet, *Margaret Graham* (ON.1004), left Amble in Northumberland in July 1999 and brought the Waveney era in Britain to a close. Her departure, at 2pm on Saturday 24 July, was formally marked by the Institution as the Waveney class was officially decommissioned. Many Coxswains who had served on board Waveneys were present at Amble to say a final farewell to the class. Frank Ide, former Poole Coxswain, Keith Stewart of Fowey, Robin Castle of Sheerness and former Newhaven Coxswain Len Patten were all in attendance. *Margaret Graham* sailed from Amble under the command of her retiring coxswain, Rodney Burge MBE, to take up a new role at Whitby as the local pilot boat, renamed *St Hilda of Whitby.*

Middle lower   Moored in Navyard Wharf at Harwich, *John Fison* (44-020) is dwarfed by her replacement, 17m Severn *Albert Brown* (ON.1202), in August 1996. (Peter Edey)

Moored at RNLI Depot, Poole, in October 1996 are *Barham* (44-021), *St Patrick* (44-014) and *John F Kennedy* (44-002), almost at the end of their operational lives.   (Nicholas Leach)

During more than three decades of service, the Waveney answered more than 7000 calls and saved over 2800 lives. The coxswains and crews who served on the boat performed many fine rescues, and this is reflected in the number of bravery medals awarded to Coxswains and crews who operated the boats: six Silver and 14 Bronze medals were won in Waveneys.

In America, the USCG developed a new 47ft motor lifeboat that was faster than the 44-footer and, like the Trent developed by the RNLI, offered improved crew protection and survivor comfort. The new 47ft lifeboat was designed to have the durability and survivability of the 44-footer while incorporating technological advances made since the early-1960s. Designed to be a multi-function vessel, it was to be used for search and rescue, law enforcement and environmental protection. The new design had a higher speed, better seakeeping and crew protection, and greater towing capacity than the 44-footer. It was also easier to operate, more comfortable and reduced crew fatigue when operating on long missions.

The replacement project began in 1986 and after refinement of the initial design, a contract to finish it was awarded to Textron Marine and Land Systems who built the prototype boat. In July 1990, CG-47200 was delivered to the 47ft MLB Test Team in Ilwaco, WA, for developmental testing and evaluation. This boat then went to Station Cape Disappointment for further evaluation in September 1990. Between April 1992 and December 1994, five pre-production boats were built for operational testing and evaluations. These were assigned to Coast Guard units on both coasts to maximize the benefits of the testing period which resulted in further refinements to the boat's design.

In November 1995, a contract was awarded to build twenty 47ft MLBs at a cost of $26M. In May 1997, the first production boat, CG-47206 was delivered to the National Motor Lifeboat School in Ilwaco to train the USCG crews. Once the new design had been accepted for service, full production of approximately 100 47-footers began and the venerable 44-foot motor lifeboats started to be replaced. Many of the replaced 44-footers were sold as part of the foreign military sales program of the US Government as they had many years of service left.

In Canada, the first 44ft lifeboats to be decommissioned were those on the Atlantic seaboard. They were replaced by 52ft Arun class lifeboats, the first of which was constructed out of fibre reinforced plastic by Halmatic Ltd, in Hampshire, with the rest constructed from aluminium in Canada. On Canada's West coast the replacement for the 44-footers involved the construction of new USCG 47ft motor lifeboats instead of Aruns, thus continuing a trend for using USCG designs going back to beginning of the 20th century. As the US boats were designed for conditions similar to those encountered in Canada, using them in Canada has many benefits, such as joint training exercises which reduce costs.

Preserved for the future

What became of the prototypes, CG-44300 and 44-001? Fortunately for those interested in lifeboats and the history of life-saving, both craft have been preserved and are displayed in the countries where they served as prototypes. CG-44300 was withdrawn from service after a serious engine breakdown was experienced during a search and rescue mission off Cape Disappointment on 29 July 1996. Although the boat was in excellent condition, the cost of repairing the damaged engine could not be justified, particularly as the 44-

Moored at Dun Laoghaire in July 1991, *Lady of Lancashire* (44-015) and *Arthur and Blanche Harris* (44-006), the latter relieving the former.   (Tony Denton)

footers were being replaced by new 47ft motor lifeboats. After a survey, CG-44300 was handed over to the Columbia River Maritime Museum in 1998, where she joined an outstanding collection of USCG rescue craft. With her equipment and accessories intact, bearing the scars of her long career with the USCG, she is to be displayed at the Museum as the centrepiece of the story of the men and women of the US Coast Guard who risk their lives. It will focus on rescues on the Columbia River bar and showcase how the USCG has succeeded in making the Columbia River a safer waterway for commercial shipping and pleasure boating.

Meanwhile the British prototype, 44-001, went to Chatham Historic Dockyard in 1997 to form part of the National Lifeboat Collection. She was kept afloat at the Museum during the first three years, moored at Thunderbolt Pier for visitors to view. In June 1999, she was taken to Poole by a team of museum volunteers to participate in the RNLI's 175th Anniversary Celebrations. She is one of the most important lifeboats of the 20th century and her preservation ensures that the significance of the 44ft design will not be forgotten.

Waveneys in New Zealand

Although no longer in service with the RNLI, many of the Waveneys built for service in the UK have continued their life-saving role on the other side of the world. Six Waveneys were sold for service with the New Zealand Volunteer Coastguard, and a further six went to the Royal Volunteer Coastal Patrol in Australia. With limited resources, these two organisations have been able to purchase the Waveneys as second-hand lifeboats relatively cheaply and as the boats were well maintained by the RNLI, and the steel hulls suffered only minimal wear, they have many years of service ahead of them. The impact of the Waveneys in Australia and New Zealand is considerable, and in both countries they have improved life-saving facilities considerably.

While specific information about which Waveneys were sold to New Zealand can be found with details of the individual lifeboats, their sale to New Zealand was an interesting development and warrants further explanation. In 1997, the Royal New Zealand Coastguard Federation (RNZCF) decided to purchase five, possibly six, Waveneys

Top **Ready for service in Australia,** *Arthur and Blanche Harris* **(44-006) moored at Souter's Shipyard, Cowes, repainted in the colours of the Royal Volunteer Coastal Patrol, Australia. (Peter Edey)**

Upper middle **Painted in Australian Coastguard livery,** *Arthur and Blanche Harris* **(44-006) and** *Faithful Forester* **(44-004) moored together at RNLI Depot, Poole, in August 1999, await shipping to their new operators. (Nicholas Leach)**

Lower middle **After service, 44-001 was used as a publicity lifeboat operating from Chatham Historic Dockyard and as such took part in the RNLI's 175th Anniversary Celebrations at Poole in June 1999. She formed part of a fleet of lifeboats and is seen here off Bournemouth Pier. (Nicholas Leach)**

Bottom **After service,** *John F Kennedy* **(44-002) was renamed** *Sarah JFK* **and, with the aft cabin removed, was used to take angling parties from her base at Newcastle. (Nicholas Leach)**

being offered for sale by the RNLI. Between them, Harold Mason and Lew Robinson of the RNZCF considered where the vessels would best be stationed, and then negotiated a bulk purchase of five Waveneys over three years.

The project was financed in part by the country's Lottery Grants Board, without whose help the project would not have been possible. The RNLI offset all costs in getting the boats to Tilbury as well as loading charges incurred at the port. P&O Nedlloyd agreed to ship the vessels free of charge, a sponsorship worth approximately NZ$400,000. They had already received excellent publicity for their free-of-charge shipping of the RNLI's 33ft Brede lifeboat *Amateur Swimming Associations* (ON.1105) to New Zealand for service with the Nelson Volunteer Coastguard, where she was renamed *Sealord Rescue*. As well as the sponsorship of P&O Nedlloyd, Port Wellington and Port Auckland container terminals provided unloading free of charge.

The first Waveney to arrive, *Wavy Line* (ON.1043), was allocated to the Mana Volunteer Coastguard. She arrived on board the container ship *Pegasus Bay* and was renamed *Nicholsons Rescue* at a commissioning ceremony on 21 May 1998. The second, *Louis Marchesi of Round Table* (ON.1045), reached New Zealand on 4 April 1999 and was allocated to Waiheke Volunteer Coastguard.

In 1999, David Acland agreed to sponsor the Waveney allocated to Kaikoura Volunteer Coastguard, *The William and Jane* (ON.1079). His gesture was made in memory of his great, great uncle John Barton Acland who came to New Zealand 130 years ago and established the Mount Peel high-country station, which the family still own and operate.

As a specific example, the acquisition of *The William and Jane* shows how important these boats were to both the communities in which they served and to the nation as a whole. *The William and Jane* was acquired for the Kaikoura Coastguard (KCG) after they lobbied to have a Waveney assigned to the area. Kaikoura is situated on the east coast of the south island of New Zealand, about half way between Cook Strait and Banks Peninsula. Kaikoura Peninsula provides the only shelter, albeit somewhat rugged, for many miles on what is a very exposed coast. The need for a lifeboat is therefore considerable.

Once allocated to KCG, *The William and Jane* left Tilbury Docks on 30 May 1999, together with a Waveney destined for Australia, as deck cargo on board the container ship *P&O Nedlloyd Palliser Bay*. She arrived in Wellington, New

Top Perhaps the Waveney to be most heavily altered after service was *Helen Turnbull* (44-009), renamed *Badger,* and seen here out of the water at Dickie's Boatyard, Bangor. (Nicholas Leach)

Upper middle Touching New Zealand water for the first time, *The William and Jane* (44-022) arrives at her new home on 16 July 1999. (Harold Mason)

Lower middle Renaming day on 12 December 1999, *Louis Marchesi of Round Table* (44-019) is christened at Matiatia Bay for service with the Waiheke Volunteer Coastguard. (Harold Mason)

Bottom Ready for service in Canada, *The White Rose of Yorkshire* (44-012) is lowered into the water at Souter's Shipyard, Cowes, 18 June 1999, in new livery. (Peter Edey)

Zealand, on 16 July 1999 and was unloaded, free of charge, by the Wellington Port Company. The KCG crew travelled to Wellington to meet *P&O Nedlloyd Palliser Bay* in the morning and were aboard the Wellington tugs *Kupe* and *Toia* which brought the ship in.

Once the ship had docked, the Waveney was lowered into the water and the KCG crew prepared her for the passage to Kaikoura the following day. Before passage to her new station, the boat was fully checked over by her new crew and by crew from Mana Coastguard, who already operated a Waveney. The passage to Kaikoura, 96 nautical miles south of Wellington, involved crossing the notorious Cook Strait then down to South Island's east coast, and to Kaikoura Peninsula.

The lifeboat arrived at Kaikoura at 4.30pm on Saturday 17 July 1999 after a relatively uneventful passage. She was subsequently slipped, anti-fouled, and had GPS and other equipment fitted before becoming operational. A berth was provided in the local Marina free of charge. The new boat's first call was to a yacht which had broken down in 50-knot winds and was blown out to sea off the Kaikoura Peninsula. The yacht was taken in tow by the lifeboat and brought to a sheltered mooring out of the heavy seas.

The formalities of the KCG's new acquisition were completed with both a church and a Maori blessing on 20 November 1999. At the ceremony, attended by RNZCG executives, local Dignitaries, sponsors, and other Coastguard units, the boat was renamed. So under a new name, with a new crew, and at a new station, another of the RNLI's Waveneys continues in her role as life-saver. Overall, the project has resulted in a dramatic improvement in rescue coverage of New Zealand's coastline and, together with those currently in service as lifeboats in Australia, has given the Waveneys a new lease of life as they are still being used as lifeboats.

Above Former RNLI Waveney *Wavy Line* (44-017), one of the Waveneys sold for service in New Zealand, seen here renamed *Trust Porirua Rescue* and in the colours of Mana Volunteer Coastguard, based on North Island. (John Jamieson)

Below Former RNLI Waveney *John Fison* (44-020), seen here renamed *Rotary Rescue* and in RNZCG colours, in the process of trying to tow a small fishing trawler which was grounded at the entrance to Raglan Harbour on New Zealand's North Island. (Waikato Times, courtesy of John Gower)

Bibliography

Dutton, Lieut Commdr W L G (1967): The Development of the 44ft USCG Steel Lifeboat, in Item No.3 in *Report on the Tenth International Lifeboat Conference held in Dinard 1967*, pp.23-25.

Fry, Eric (1975): *Lifeboat Design and Development* (David & Charles, London).

MacDonald, S et al (1975): RNLI Lifeboats in the 1970s, Royal Institute of Naval Architects, pp.301-324.

Morris, Jeff (1986): *Lists of British Life-boats, Part III: Motor Lifeboats*.

— (1995): *The Story of the Ramsgate Lifeboats*.

— (1996): *The History of the Eyemouth Lifeboats*.

— (1996): *The History of the Sheerness Lifeboats*.

— (1997): *The Story of the Whitby Lifeboats*.

Noble, Dennis (2000): *Lifeboat Sailors: Disasters, Rescues and the perilous future of the Coast Guard's Small Boat Stations* (Brassey's, Washington DC).

Smith, Richard R (1963): Operational Characteristics of the United States Coast Guard 44-foot Motor Lifeboat, Item No.6 in *Report on the Ninth International Lifeboat Conference held in Edinburgh*, June 1963, pp.66-70.

Wilkinson, William D (1998): The US Coast Guard 44-foot Motor Lifeboat, in *Quarterdeck*, newsletter for Columbia River Maritime Museum, Vol.24, No.1, Winter 1998.

Witter, Robert W, Lt Cdr (1963): Design and Construction of the United States Coast Guard 44-foot Motor Lifeboat, Item No.5 in *Report on the Ninth International Lifeboat Conference held in Edinburgh*, June 1963, pp.51-65.

Op No	ON	Year	Builder	ORN*	Cost	Engines	Page
44-001	—	1964	USCG Yard, Curtis Bay	—	—	2x200hp Cummins 1973– 2x250hp Ford Mermaid 595T 1982– 2x203hp Caterpillar 3208	32
44-002	1001	1966	Brooke Marine	309880	£33,000	2x215hp Cummins V6 1983– 2x203hp Caterpillar D3208	36
44-003	1002	1967	Brooke Marine	309891	£33,361	2x215hp Cummins V6 1981– 2x203hp Caterpillar D3208	38
44-004	1003	1967	Brooke Marine	334667	£35,000	2x215hp Cummins V6 1982– 2x203hp Caterpillar D3208	41
44-005	1004	1967	Brooke Marine	334656	£37,838	2x215hp Cummins V6 1982– 2x203hp Caterpillar D3208	44
44-006	1005	1968	Brooke Marine	335723	£35,000	2x215hp Cummins V6 1979– 2x203hp Caterpillar D3208	46
44-007	1006	1968	Brooke Marine	335724	£34,386	2x215hp Cummins V6 1982– 2x203hp Caterpillar D3208	49
44-008	1026	1974	Groves & Guttridge	363582	£100,000	2x260hp General Motors GM 8V-53	52
44-009	1027	1974	Groves & Guttridge	363584	£100,000	2x260hp General Motors GM 8V-53	54
44-010	1028	1974	Groves & Guttridge	366146	£100,000	2x260hp General Motors GM 8V-53	57
44-011	1029	1974	Groves & Guttridge	363580	£81,000	2x260hp General Motors GM 8V-53	59
44-012	1033	1974	Groves & Guttridge	363583	£79,018	2x260hp General Motors GM 8V-53	62
44-013	1034	1974	Groves & Guttridge	365983	£100,000	2x260hp General Motors GM 8V-53	64
44-014	1035	1974	Groves & Guttridge	366147	£100,000	2x260hp General Motors GM 8V-53	66
44-015	1036	1975	Groves & Guttridge	365998	£85,967	2x260hp General Motors GM 8V-53	68
44-016	1042	1976	Bideford Shipyard	377149	£130,000	2x250hp Ford Mermaid 595T 1981– 2x250hp Caterpillar D3208T	70
44-017	1043	1976	Bideford Shipyard	377151	£174,688	2x250hp Ford Mermaid 595T 1978– 2x250hp Caterpillar D3208T 1980– 2x250hp Caterpillar D3208T	73
44-018	1044	1977	Bideford Shipyard	377263	£122,000	2x250hp Ford Mermaid 595T 1982– 2x250hp Caterpillar D3208T	76
44-019	1045	1977	Bideford Shipyard	377343	£150,000	2x250hp Ford Mermaid 595T 1981– 2x250hp Caterpillar D3208T	78
44-020	1060	1980	Fairey Marine	390694	£260,000	2x250hp Caterpillar 3208T	80
44-021	1065	1980	Fairey Marine	705487	£260,000	2x250hp Caterpillar 3208T	82
44-022	1079	1982	Fairey Marine	703255	£319,940	2x250hp Caterpillar D3208T	84

*ORN is the official registration number allocated to vessels by the Department of Trade.

Abbreviations used in the movements lists

CT	Crew training	ON	Official number	R	Repairs
dis	display	RE	Re-engined	Sh Yd	Shipyard
ER	Emergency Relief	rlvd	relieved by	SRT	Self-righting trials
ET	Evaluation trials	rlvg	relieving	std	Stored
HC	Hull clean	S	Survey	T	Trials
I	Inspection	S&R	Survey and repairs	TSD	Temporary Station Duty
M	Maintenance	sl	station lifeboat	7/2	launches/lives

Key information

Official Number	Not allocated
Year built	1964
Builder	United States CG Yard
Yard No.	—-
Cost	—-
Weight	16t14

Donor

Bought from the US Coastguard, purchased from RNLI General Funds in 1964, brought to the London Docks by the steamship *Alaunia* on 19 May 1964.

Stations

	Years on station	Record
Trials around Britain	1964 – 1967	7/9
Relief	1 Feb 1967 – 6 Mar 1997	291/100

Movements

19.5.1964-20.5.1964	Berthed at King George Fifth Dock after arriving from USA
20.5.1964-21.5.1964	Passage trials
21.5.1964-27.5.1964	Wm Osborne, Littlehampton (on view to Committee of Management)
25.5.1964	Littlehampton (viewed by the Committee of Management)
26.5.1964	Littlehampton (press day)
27.5.1964-30.5.1964	Passage to Appledore
30.5.1964-2.6.1964	Appledore (T)
2.6.1964-5.6.1964	Passage back to Solent
5.6.1964-20.9.1964	Wm Osborne, Littlehampton (T)
11.6.1964-28.6.1964	Solent and Channel Isles (T)
29.6.1964-5.7.1964	Littlehampton (T)
6.7.1964-31.7.1964	Passage to Humber and North-East
31.7.1964-1.8.1964	Returned to Littlehampton (R)
1.8.1964-20.8.1964	Various trials and familiarisation in Solent area (4/6)
7.8.1964	Visited by HRH Duke of Edinburgh, Prince Charles and Princess Anne
20.9.1964-11.12.1964	Passage and evaluation trials round Britain from Cowes westward to the south-west and Wales, Ireland, Scotland, Northern Isles, Eastern England and back to Littlehampton; while in Orkney/Shetland, delegation of 3 from the North and South Holland Lifeboat Society went afloat in her
11.12.1964-20.1.1965	Wm Osborne, Littlehampton (T)
20.1.1965-10.2.1965	Passage visit to Holland (while at Ryde Pier performed a service on 4.2.1965)
10.2.1965-1.2.1967	Wm Osborne, Littlehampton (T; service on 26.3.1966, saved yacht off Beachy Head, and 3 lives)
1.2.1967-3.2.1967	Passage to Barry Dock
3.2.1967-3.6.1968	Barry Dock (rlvg ON.806: 2/0)
3.6.1968-19.9.1968	Clovelly (rlvg ON.987: 9/7)
19.9.1968-28.9.1968	Passage to Dun Laoghaire
28.9.1968-14.12.1968	Dun Laoghaire (rlvg ON.1001: 1/0)
14.12.1968-6.1.1969	Passage to Great Yarmouth & Gorleston
6.1.1969-11.4.1969	Great Yarmouth & Gorleston (rlvg ON.1002: 1/0)
11.4.1969-20.4.1969	Passage to Harwich (T)
20.4.1969-5.8.1969	Harwich (rlvg ON.1004: 1/0)
5.8.1969-1.9.1969	Sheerness (rlvg ON.1017: 7/4)
1.9.1969-7.9.1969	Passage to Clovelly
7.9.1969-20.9.1969	Clovelly (rlvg ON.987)
20.9.1969-8.11.1969	Barry Dock (rlvg ON.1005: 5/0)
8.11.1969-2.12.1969	Mashford's Bt Yd, Plymouth (ER)
2.12.1969-4.12.1969	Passage to Sheerness
4.12.1969-1.2.1970	Sheerness (ET, Sheerness station to be established 1.1970)
1.2.1970-2.2.1970	Passage to Dun Laoghaire
2.2.1970-20.3.1970	Dun Laoghaire (rlvg ON.1001: 0/0)
20.3.1970-22.3.1970	Passage to Sheerness
22.3.1970-29.7.1970	Sheerness (ET, ER)
29.7.1970-31.7.1970	Passage to Clovelly
31.7.1970-3.9.1970	Clovelly (rlvg ON.987: 1/8)
3.9.1970-5.9.1970	Passage to Harwich (on 3.9.1970 gave help to a dinghy and landed 2)

When she arrived in the United Kingdom, 44-001 had a white superstructure, and this was retained during the subsequent trials around the coast. (RNLI)

After evaluation trials, 44-001 was allocated to the Relief Fleet and as such served at many stations. She is seen here at Harwich in August 1986. (Nicholas Leach)

5.9.1970-20.11.1970	Harwich (rlvg ON.1004: 4/0)
20.11.1970-23.11.1970	Passage to Barry Dock
23.11.1970-31.3.1971	Barry Dock (rlvg ON.1005: 2/0)
31.3.1971-2.4.1971	Passage to Littlehampton
2.4.1971-30.6.1971	Wm Osborne, Littlehampton (S, R)
7.8.1971-31.8.1971	Dover (rlvg ON.1003: 3/2)
31.8.1971-1.6.1972	Harwich (rlvg ON.1004: 3/0)
6.6.1972-31.10.1972	Clovelly (rlvg ON.987: 3/5)
2.11.1972-3.1.1973	Barry Dock (rlvg ON.1005: 1/0)
3.1.1973-3.1.1974	Mashford's Bt Yd, Plymouth (S, ER)
3.1.1974-5.1.1974	Passage to Great Yarmouth & Gorleston
5.1.1974-30.6.1974	Great Yarmouth & Gorleston (rlvg ON.1002: 8/2)
30.6.1974-1.7.1974	Passage to Harwich
1.7.1974-31.1.1975	Harwich (rlvg ON.1004: 9/14)
31.1.1975-1.2.1975	Passage to Dover
1.2.1975-31.5.1975	Dover (rlvg ON.1003: 2/0)
31.5.1975-30.6.1975	Sheerness (rlvg ON.1027: 2/0)
30.6.1975-9.7.1975	Passage to Eyemouth
9.7.1975-31.10.1975	Eyemouth (rlvg ON.1026: 1/0)
31.10.1975-13.11.1975	Passage to Harwich
13.11.1975-4.4.1976	Harwich (rlvg ON.1004: 5/0)
4.4.1976-13.4.1976	Fletchers Bt Yd, Lowestoft (I, M)
13.4.1976-14.4.1976	Passage to Whitby
14.4.1976-2.6.1976	Whitby (rlvg ON.1033: 3/6)
2.6.1976-3.6.1976	Passage to Dover
3.6.1976-24.10.1976	Dover (rlvg ON.1003: 14/9)
24.10.1976-17.12.1976	Sheerness (rlvg ON.1027: 7/0)
17.12.1976-5.1.1977	Brown's Bt Yd, Rowhedge (ER at Brightlingsea)
5.1.1977-8.1.1977	Passage to Eyemouth
8.1.1977-13.3.1977	Eyemouth (rlvg ON.1026: 3/0)
13.3.1977-14.3.1977	Passage to Great Yarmouth & Gorleston
14.3.1977-17.3.1977	Great Yarmouth & Gorleston (rlvg ON.1002: 0/0)
17.3.1977-25.3.1977	Fletchers Bt Yd, Lowestoft (R)
25.3.1977-10.6.1977	Great Yarmouth & Gorleston (rlvg ON.1002: 6/0)
10.6.1977-11.6.1977	Passage to Hartlepool
11.6.1977-27.6.1977	Hartlepool (CT, ON.1044 sent 21.6.1977 as new lifeboat)
27.6.1977-28.6.1977	Passage to Humber
28.6.1977-10.7.1977	Humber (rlvg ON.1052: 1/0)
10.7.1977-20.7.1977	Hartlepool (rlvg ON.1044: 0/0)
20.7.1977-22.7.1977	Passage to Cardnell's Bt Yd
22.7.1977-15.10.1977	Cardnell's Bt Yd, Maylandsea (S & ER)
15.10.1977-23.1.1978	Harwich (rlvg ON.1004: 5/0)
23.1.1978-3.4.1978	Sheerness (rlvg ON.1027: 0/0)
3.4.1978-25.6.1978	Ramsgate (rlvg ON.1042: 2/0)
25.6.1978-28.6.1978	Passage to St Helier
28.6.1978-23.7.1978	St Helier (rlvg ON.1034: 1/2)
23.7.1978-24.7.1978	Passage to Falmouth Boat Co
24.7.1978-16.8.1978	Falmouth Boat Co, Falmouth (R)
16.8.1978-10.6.1979	Falmouth (rlvg ON.1031: 13/0)
10.6.1979-27.4.1980	Falmouth Boat Co, Falmouth (S)
27.4.1980-28.4.1980	Passage to Barry Dock
28.4.1980-11.6.1980	Barry Dock (rlvg ON.1018: 1/0)
11.6.1980-12.6.1980	Passage to Falmouth Boat Co
12.6.1980-3.7.1980	Falmouth Boat Co, Falmouth (M)
3.7.1980-5.7.1980	Passage to Barry Dock
5.7.1980-16.12.1980	Barry Dock (rlvg ON.1018: 8/3)
16.12.1980-8.1.1981	Passage to RNLI Depot, Poole (to Padstow for Christmas recess, remained there until 6.1.1981 when resumed passage: 0/0)
8.1.1981-13.2.1981	RNLI Depot, Poole Depot (std)
13.2.1981-26.9.1981	FBM Marine Ltd. Cowes (RE, T)
26.9.1981-29.9.1981	Passage to Newhaven
29.9.1981-25.5.1982	Newhaven (rlvg ON.1045: 22/12)
25.5.1982-26.5.1982	Passage to Great Yarmouth & Gorleston
26.5.1982-12.6.1982	Great Yarmouth & Gorleston (rlvg ON.1065: 1/0)
12.6.1982-23.6.1982	Brown's Bt Yd, Rowhedge (I)
23.6.1982-31.10.1982	Sheerness (rlvg ON.1027: 16/4)
31.10.1982-2.12.1982	Wm Osborne, Littlehampton (R)
2.12.1982-2.7.1983	Dover (rlvg ON.1031: 7/0)
2.7.1983-7.7.1983	Passage to Harwich (via Ramsgate)
7.7.1983-30.10.1983	Harwich (rlvg ON.1060: 1/0)
30.10.1983-12.3.1984	Great Yarmouth & Gorleston (rlvg ON.1065: 4/0)
12.3.1984-18.8.1984	Crescent Marine, Otterham Qy (M)
18.8.1984-20.8.1984	Passage to St Helier
20.8.1984-10.12.1984	St Helier (rlvg ON.1034: 7/3)
10.12.1984-12.12.1984	Passage to Sheerness
12.12.1984-8.7.1985	Sheerness (rlvg ON.1027: 15/5)
8.7.1985-9.7.1985	Crescent Marine, Otterham Qy (R)
9.7.1985-5.11.1985	Harwich (rlvg ON.1060: 5/4)
5.11.1985-14.11.1985	Whisstocks Bt Yd, Woodbridge (ER)
14.11.1985-16.11.1985	Passage to Hartlepool
16.11.1985-29.11.1985	Hartlepool (rlvg ON.1044: 0/0)
29.11.1985-1.12.1985	Passage to Whisstocks
1.12.1985-2.3.1987	Whisstocks Bt Yd, Woodbridge (ER, std)
2.3.1987-4.3.1987	Passage to Yarmouth (IOW)
4.3.1987-10.8.1987	Yarmouth (rlvg ON.1053: 9/7)
10.8.1987-11.8.1987	Passage to Whisstocks
11.8.1987-21.10.1987	Whisstocks Bt Yd, Woodbridge (M, ER)
21.10.1987-22.10.1987	Passage to Crescent Marine
22.10.1987-30.1.1988	Crescent Marine, Otterham Quay (R, M)
30.1.1988-1.2.1988	Passage to Tynemouth
1.2.1988-18.2.1988	Tynemouth (rlvg ON.1061: 0/0)
18.2.1988-21.2.1988	Passage to Crescent Marine
21.2.1988-12.9.1988	Crescent Marine, Otterham Qy (S)
12.9.1988-14.9.1988	Passage to Branksea Marine
14.9.1988-10.10.1988	Branksea Marine, Wareham (M)
10.10.1988-16.10.1988	Alderney (rlvg ON.1045: 0/0)
16.10.1988-2.11.1988	RNLI Depot, Poole (ER)
2.11.1988-9.7.1989	Poole (rlvg ON.1089: 14/0)
9.7.1989-19.9.1989	RNLI Depot, Poole (ER)
19.9.1989-20.9.1989	Passage to Ramsgate
20.9.1989-13.10.1989	Ramsgate (rlvg ON.1042: 0/0)
13.10.1989-6.2.1990	Crescent Marine, Otterham Qy (S)
6.2.1990-23.4.1990	Sheerness (rlvg ON.1027: 9/0)
23.4.1990-25.4.1990	Passage to Eyemouth (service: 1/0)
25.4.1990-23.10.1990	Eyemouth (rlvg ON.1026: 6/2)
23.10.1990-25.10.1990	Passage to Crescent Marine (via

	Scarborough, Lowestoft: 1/0)
25.10.1990-6.12.1991	Crescent Marine, Rainham (S)
6.12.1991-16.1.1992	Sheerness (rlvg ON.1027: 5/0)
16.1.1992-1.3.1993	Crescent Marine, Otterham Quay (ER, std)
1.3.1993-4.3.1993	Passage to Hartlepool
4.3.1993-13.8.1993	Hartlepool (rlvg ON.1044 after capsize)
13.8.1993-16.8.1993	Passage to Eastbourne
16.8.1993-15.11.1993	Langney Marine, Eastbourne (S)
15.11.1993-18.1.1994	Fowey (rlvg ON.1028)
18.1.1994-19.1.1994	Passage to Poole
19.1.1994-30.1.1994	RNLI Depot, Poole (std)
30.1.1994-31.1.1994	Passage to Sheerness
31.1.1994-23.5.1994	Crescent Marine, Otterham Quay (ER, std at Crescent Bt Yd)
23.5.1994-25.5.1994	Passage (via Sheerness 23.5.94 and Newhaven 24.5.94)
25.5.1994-27.5.1994	RNLI Depot, Poole (std)
27.5.1994	Passage to Alderney
27.5.1994-8.7.1994	Alderney (Relief during D-Day Landing Review 5-7.6.1994, ON.1180 based at Ouisterham)
8.7.1994-11.8.1994	RNLI Depot, Poole (ER)
11.8.1994-3.9.1994	Poole (rlvg ON.1089)
3.9.1994-10.10.1994	RNLI Depot, Poole (ER)
10.10.1994-26.10.1994	Torbay (rlvg ON.1086)
26.10.1994-31.10.1994	Passage (via Yarmouth 27.10.94, Newhaven 28.10.94, Ramsgate 29.10.94 and Sheerness 30.10.94)
31.10.1994-18.5.1995	Crescent Marine, Otterham Quay (ER, std)
18.5.1995-23.5.1995	Otterham Quay (awaiting passage)
23.5.1995-25.5.1995	Passage to Poole (via Dover 24.5.95 and Newhaven 25.5.95)
25.5.1995-27.5.1995	RNLI Depot, Poole (std)
27.5.1995-4.9.1995	Exmouth (rlvg ON.1045)
4.9.1995-10.9.1995	Passage (via Plymouth 5.9.95, Newlyn 6-7.9.95, Padstow 8.9.95, Fishguard 9.9.95)
10.9.1995-6.12.1995	Arklow (relieving ON.1029)
6.12.1995-21.12.1995	Passage (via Milford Haven 6.12.95, Padstow 7.12.95, Newlyn 8.12.95, Plymouth 9.12.95, Exmouth 10-18.12.95, Yarmouth 19.12.95, Newhaven 20.12.95, Dover 21.12.95)
22.12.1995-6.3.1997	Otterham Quay (std, ER)
6.3.1997-6.3.1997	Passage to Chatham
6.3.1997-	Chatham Historic Dockyard (dis); based at Chatham has served as a publicity lifeboat as follows:
21.8.1997-25.8.1997	Chatham Maritime Festival
5.11.1997-13.3.1998	Anchor Wharf, Chatham (HC, std)
13.6.1998-14.6.1998	Kingston-on-Thames Regatta
4.7.1998-5.7.1998	Ramsgate Ships Open Day
25.7.1998-25.7.1998	Whitstable Oyster Festival
8.3.1999-1.4.1999	Denton Shiprepairers (I, HC)
3.4.1999	University Boat Race, Putney
16.5.1999	Escorted HMS *Cavalier* into river Medway
29.5.1999	Escorted Dunkirk Little Ships into river Medway
12.6.1999-13.6.1999	Kingston-on-Thames Regatta
16.6.1999-20.6.1999	Passage to Poole (via Ramsgate, Newhaven)
20.6.1999-26.6.1999	Poole (RNLI 175th Anniversary)
25.6.1999-26.6.1999	Passage to Ramsgate
26.6.1999-3.7.1999	Ramsgate Marina (std)
3.7.1999	Passage to Chatham
26.5.2000-29.5.2000	Chatham Navy Days

Notable rescue

The prototype Waveney, 44-001, was operated as a Relief lifeboat for more then three decades and performed many rescues at the stations she served. The most notable of these took place on 6 October 1990 when she was on relief duty at Eyemouth. That day Scotland's south-east coast experienced hurricane-force winds gusting to 100mph, accompanied by heavy rain with waves up to 20 feet high running at the entrance to the harbour.

After some divers were caught out by the storm, the lifeboat crew were summoned. However, not all responded as telephone lines were down and the maroons could not be heard in the storm. Neither Coxswain nor Second Coxswain could be contacted, so Assistance Mechanic James Dougal

On her coastal tour, 44-001 seen at Padstow on 29 May 1964 on display in the harbour. (Grahame Farr)

44-001 setting out from Newhaven on service on 24 October 1981 to help a disabled trawler. (Jeff Morris)

took command as Acting Coxswain. At 4.49pm, 44-001 slipped her moorings and headed through the appalling conditions at the harbour entrance out to sea, pounding head-on into the huge waves.

A course was set for St Abbs, where the divers had been reported, but speed had to be reduced as 35 foot seas were encountered. The lifeboat arrived off St Abbs harbour at 5.15pm, where together with the Dunbar lifeboat and using the searchlight, Acting Coxswain Dougal took 44-001 close to rocks to look for the divers, with all crew on deck secured by their lifelines. At 5.20pm two divers were spotted just north of Ebb Carr Rocks. The lifeboat was manoeuvred towards them, and after two attempts a line was thrown to them. They were pulled on board the lifeboat where they were treated for shock and hypothermia.

The two divers were suffering from severe seasickness and so an attempt was made by Acting Coxswain Dougal to land them at St Abbs. However, conditions at the harbour there were too severe to safely et the lifeboat through the narrow entrance. Together with the Dunbar lifeboat, 44-001 carried out searches for two other missing divers but without success and at 7.45pm the search was abandoned.

The two lifeboats made for Burnmouth but as all the harbour lights were out there local fisherman, J. Johnston, arranged for two cars, with their headlights full on, to be positioned to indicate the correct course and enable the lifeboat to enter the harbour. Both boats safely negotiated the entrance to Burnmouth harbour and were moored. At 8.45pm news was received that the other two divers had been washed ashore north of Eyemouth and were safe.

For this outstanding service, Acting Coxswain Dougal was awarded the Silver medal for taking the lifeboat to sea despite the port of Eyemouth being closed due to the appalling conditions. The Thanks on Vellum was accorded to each member of the crew, Acting Mechanic John Buchan, Acting Assistant mechanic David Collin, and crew members George Walker, Robert Walker, Joseph Walker and Alistair Crombie. Despite being more than 20 years old when this service took place, 44-001 performed superbly throughout the rescue and ensured its successful outcome.

Disposal

44-001 was withdrawn from service on 9 January 1996. In March 1997, she became part of the Historic Lifeboat Collection, and was taken to Chatham Dockyard. She was used as a floating exhibit at the Dockyard, and was taken to various towns in the locality supporting fund-raising events, notably Kingston-on-Thames, Ramsgate and Whitstable. In June 1999 she was part of the gathering of historic and international lifeboats at Poole held as part of the RNLI's 175th Anniversary Celebrations. For the event she was manned by a group of volunteers from Chatham Dockyard. In May 2000 she was on display at Chatham Navy Days. This was her last official engagement before being lifted out of the water to become part of the static exhibition at Chatham's No.4 slipway.

After the capsize of *The Scout* (44-018) in 1993, 44-001 served at Hartlepool on relief duty. While at Hartlepool, she attended Teesmouth Lifeboat Day on 4 July 1993 and is seen here at speed in the river Tees. (Steve Dutton)

Above Out of the water at RNLI Depot, Poole, awaiting passage in October 1994, 44-001 seen 30 years after first arriving to Britain. (Nicholas Leach)

Below One of the historic lifeboats at the RNLI's 175th Anniversary Celebrations in June 1999, 44-001 passes the crowds on Poole Quay manned by a crew of volunteers from Chatham Historic Dockyard. (Nicholas Leach)

Key information

Official Number	1001
Year built	1967
Builder	Brooke Marine, Lowestoft
Yard No.	B 348
Cost	£33,000
Weight	17t15

Donor

Provided by a legacy left by the late Miss Charlotte M H Gibson, Wellington, Somerset, and RNLI Funds.
Named on 12 August 1967 at Dun Laoghaire by Mrs de Courcy Ireland, wife of the station's Honorary Secretary; dedicated by the Right Reverend Monsignor P Boylam.

Stations

Stations	Years on station	Record
Dun Laoghaire	May 1967 –Apr 1990	238/161
Relief	Apr 1990 –1996	72/10

Movements

1.1967	Displayed at Earl's Court Boat Show, London
1.4.1967-25.4.1967	Groves & Guttridge (T)
25.4.1967-2.5.1967	Passage to Dun Laoghaire
2.5.1967-16.5.1967	Dun Laoghaire (CT)
16.5.1967-26.5.1967	Passage (rlvd by ON.814)
26.5.1967-28.9.1968	Dun Laoghaire (sl)
28.9.1968-30.9.1968	Passage to Groves & Guttridge
30.9.1968-14.12.1968	Groves & Guttridge (rlvd by 44-001)
14.12.1968-1.2.1970	Dun Laoghaire (sl)
1.2.1970-20.3.1970	Tyrells Bt Yd, Arklow (rlvd by 44-001)
20.3.1970-24.6.1971	Dun Laoghaire (sl)
7.7.1971-3.9.1971	Tyrells Bt Yd, Arklow (rlvd by ON.814)
3.9.1971-19.9.1974	Dun Laoghaire (sl)
19.9.1974-20.4.1975	Tyrells Bt Yd, Arklow (S, rlvd by ON.1005)
20.4.1975-14.5.1976	Dun Laoghaire (sl)
14.5.1976-24.7.1976	Tyrells Bt Yd, Arklow (S, rlvd by ON.1005)
24.7.1976-18.4.1978	Dun Laoghaire (sl)
18.4.1978-5.8.1978	Tyrells Bt Yd, Arklow (S, rlvd by ON.849)
5.8.1978-22.4.1980	Dun Laoghaire (sl)
22.4.1980-24.9.1980	Tyrells Bt Yd, Arklow (S, rlvd by ON.1004)
24.9.1980-2.6.1982	Dun Laoghaire (sl)
2.6.1982-9.6.1982	Tyrells Bt Yd, Arklow (R, rlvd by ON.1002)
9.6.1982-21.8.1982	Dun Laoghaire (sl)
21.8.1982-19.10.1983	Holyhead Boatyard (RE, rlvd by ON.1004)
19.10.1983-21.10.1983	Passage to Dun Laoghaire
21.10.1983-9.12.1985	Dun Laoghaire (sl)
9.12.1985-12.5.1986	Tyrells Bt Yd, Arklow (rlvd by ON.1005)
12.5.1986-21.12.1987	Dun Laoghaire (sl)
21.12.1987-7.5.1988	Tyrells Bt Yd, Arklow (rlvd by ON.1005)
7.5.1988-7.9.1988	Dun Laoghaire (sl)
7.9.1988-10.9.1988	Tyrells Bt Yd, Arklow (rlvd by ON.1005)
10.9.1988-18.3.1989	Dun Laoghaire (sl)
18.3.1989-27.5.1989	Tyrells Bt Yd, Arklow (rlvd by ON.1005)
27.5.1989-1.4.1990	Dun Laoghaire (sl)
1.4.1990-4.4.1990	Passage to Buckie
4.4.1990-24.7.1990	Herd & Mackenzie, Buckie (S, to Relief Fleet)
24.7.1990-16.11.1990	Invergordon (rlvg ON.1033: 7/3)
16.11.1990-18.11.1990	Passage to Amble (via Buckie and Montrose)
18.11.1990-19.12.1990	Marshall Branson, Amble (S)
19.12.1990-11.4.1991	Hartlepool (rlvg ON.1044: 2/0)
11.4.1991-16.6.1991	Sunderland (rlvg ON.1043: 3/0)
16.6.1991-10.10.1991	Marshall Branson, Amble (S)
10.10.1991-13.12.1991	Amble (rlvg ON.1004: 2/1)
13.12.1991-6.1.1992	Marshall Branson, Amble (ER)
6.1.1992-22.2.1992	Blyth (rlvg ON.1079: 0/0)

The first Waveney built by the RNLI, *John F Kennedy* was the centrepiece of the RNLI stand at the Earl's Court Boat Show in January 1967. (Jeff Morris)

Stationed at Dun Laoghaire for more than two decades, *John F Kennedy* seen at moorings in the harbour, close to the Mail Boat Pier, on 14 May 1986. (Tony Denton)

22.2.1992-21.3.1992	Amble Bt Co, Amble (ER)
21.3.1992-27.3.1992	Tynemouth (rlvg ON.1061: 0/0)
27.3.1992-24.6.1992	Hartlepool (rlvg ON.1044: 4/0)
24.6.1992-13.9.1992	Sunderland (rlvg ON.1043: 8/0)
13.9.1992-13.11.1992	Marshall Branson, Amble (S, ER)
13.11.1992-21.12.1992	Amble (rlvg ON.1004: 2/1)
21.12.1992-6.2.1993	Marshall Branson, Amble (std)
6.2.1993-10.4.1993	Eyemouth (rlvg ON.1026: 2/0)
10.4.1993-7.6.1993	Blyth (rlvg ON.1079: 1/0)
7.6.1993-23.6.1993	Amble Marina (std)
23.6.1993-1.7.1993	Sunderland (rlvg ON.1043)
1.7.1993-7.8.1993	Sunderland (std, ON.1043 back on service 30.6.93)
7.8.1993-17.8.1993	Marshall Branson, Amble (std, ER)
17.8.1993-20.11.1993	Sunderland (rlvg ON.1043: 5/0)
20.11.1993-27.1.1994	Amble Bt Co, Amble (S)
27.1.1994-15.4.1994	Amble (rlvg ON.1004)
15.4.1994-16.4.1994	Amble Marina
16.4.1994-10.6.1994	Eyemouth (rlvg ON.1026)
10.6.1994-13.8.1994	Blyth (rlvg ON.1079)
13.8.1994-11.10.1994	Hartlepool (rlvg ON.1044)
11.10.1994-21.1.1995	Sunderland (rlvg ON.1043)
21.1.1995-23.1.1995	Passage (via Tynemouth, detained due to poor weather conditions)
23.1.1995-24.3.1995	Marshall Branson Bt Yd, Amble (S)
24.3.1995-27.5.1995	Amble (rlvg ON.1004)
27.5.1995-24.6.1995	Amble Bt Co, Amble (R)
24.6.1995-26.6.1995	Passage to Eyemouth
26.6.1995-9.9.1995	Eyemouth (rlvg ON.1026)
9.9.1995-8.12.1995	Blyth (rlvg ON.1079)
8.12.1995-13.1.1996	Amble Bt Co, Amble (R)
13.1.1996-25.3.1996	Hartlepool (rlvg ON.1044)
25.3.1996-31.7.1996	Sunderland (rlvg ON.1043)
31.7.1996-18.8.1996	Hartlepool (R, HC)
18.8.1996-19.8.1996	Passage to RNLI Depot, Poole (final passage, ovnt Scarborough)
19.8.1996-22.8.1996	Passage to RNLI Depot, Poole (via Lowestoft 19.8.95, Dover 20.8.95, Newhaven 21.8.95)
22.8.1996-16.9.1997	RNLI Depot, Poole (on sale list)
16.9.1997	Sold (departed RNLI Depot, Poole for Newcastle-upon-Tyne)

Notable rescue

On 14 October 1980 the Honorary Secretary of Dun Laoghaire lifeboat station was asked if an injured seaman could be taken off the Norwegian bulk carrier *Blix*. The crew and honorary medical advisor, Dr Niall Webb, assembled at 11.30pm and 15 minutes later *John F Kennedy* launched on service under Coxswain/Mechanic Eric Offer.

The lifeboat headed for the rendezvous position four miles east of Dun Laoghaire in a force 6 wind with rough seas. *Blix* finally anchored just before 2.00am on 15 October, but getting the lifeboat alongside proved very difficult in the heavy swell. A pilot ladder was lowered over the carrier's starboard quarter, the lifeboat was brought alongside and Dr Webb jumped from the bow to the ladder. It was a long climb of more than 30 feet to *Blix's* deck.

The injured seaman, suffering from a fractured leg and rib, was tended by Dr Webb and then secured in a Neil Robinson stretch. At 2.35am he was transferred to the lifeboat and, under the supervision of Second Coxswain Joseph Lawless, was taken down into the after cabin. The lifeboat returned for Dr Webb, but conditions made the transfer extremely difficult. After several unsuccessful attempts to take him off the doctor had to jump onto the lifeboat on the instruction of the Second Coxswain.

At 2.45am the lifeboat set off for her station, where she arrived at 3.05am, and landed the injured man who was taken to St Vincent's Hospital. For this rescue, a special doctor's vellum was presented to Dr Webb, and a collective letter of appreciation signed by the RNLI Director, Rear Admiral W. J. Graham, was sent to Coxswain Offer and his crew for their part in this service.

Disposal

John F Kennedy was placed on the sale list on 22 August 1996 and sold in August 1996 to Alan Skinner, Newcastle-upon-Tyne. Kept at Davy Bank, Newcastle, her aft cabin was removed to make a larger working area aft while the wheelhouse was enlarged. Renamed *Sarah JFK*, she has been certified and licensed to carry 12 passengers on sea angling up to 60 miles offshore, and is operated out of North Shields Fish Quay and Mill Dam, South Shields, on the river Tyne.

Above On relief duty, *John F Kennedy* moored alongside the pontoon at Blyth in July 1994. (Nicholas Leach)

Below On relief duty at Hartlepool, *John F Kennedy* attending Redcar Lifeboat Day in June 1992. (Steve Dutton)

Key information

Official Number	1002
Year built	1967
Builder	Brooke Marine, Lowestoft
Yard No.	B 349
Cost	£33,361
Weight	17t9

Donor

Gift of Mr and Mrs T G Bedwell, named after a settlement in Rhodesia where shey once lived. Named on 17 May 1967 at Gorleston-on-Sea by Mrs Bedwell.

Stations

Station	Years on station	Record
Great Yarmouth & Gorleston	19 Aug 1967 – May 1980	234/71
Relief	May 1980 – 1997	240/90

Movements

19.8.1967-6.1.1969	Great Yarmouth & Gorleston (sl)
6.1.1969-11.4.1969	Fletchers Bt Yd, Lowestoft (rlvd by 44-001)
11.4.1969-3.5.1971	Great Yarmouth & Gorleston (sl)
3.5.1971-25.7.1971	Fletchers Bt Yd, Lowestoft (rlvd by ON.819)
25.7.1971-7.1.1974	Great Yarmouth & Gorleston (sl)
7.1.1974-24.6.1974	Fletchers Bt Yd, Lowestoft (S, rlvd by 44-001)
24.6.1974-14.3.1977	Great Yarmouth & Gorleston (sl)
14.3.1977-10.6.1977	Fletchers Bt Yd, Lowestoft (rlvd by 44-001)
10.6.1977-21.4.1979	Great Yarmouth & Gorleston (sl)
21.4.1979-20.6.1979	Fletchers Bt Yd, Lowestoft (rlvd by ON.910)
20.6.1979-24.6.1979	Great Yarmouth & Gorleston (sl)
24.6.1979-29.9.1979	Fletchers Bt Yd, Lowestoft (rlvd by ON.910)
29.9.1979-30.5.1980	Great Yarmouth & Gorleston (sl, replaced by ON.1065 on 30.5.1980 and allocated to Relief Fleet)
30.5.1980-31.5.1980	Great Yarmouth & Gorleston (ER)
31.5.1980-16.6.1980	Harwich (rlvg ON.1060: 0/0)
16.6.1980-22.6.1980	Passage to Birkenhead
22.6.1980-9.4.1981	Holyhead Bt Yd, Holyhead (S)
9.4.1981-13.10.1982	Troon (rlvg ON.1006: 41/28)
13.10.1982-2.12.1982	Appledore Shipyard (std, ER)
2.12.1982-17.4.1983	Donaghadee (rlvg ON.1005: 1/0)
28.4.1983-30.7.1983	Fleetwood (rlvg ON.1036: 4/5)
6.9.1983-9.9.1983	Passage to St Helier
9.9.1983-14.5.1984	St Helier (rlvg ON.1034: 10/5)
14.5.1984-23.5.1984	St Peter Port (rlvg ON.1025: 0/0)
23.5.1984-1.6.1984	RNLI Depot, Poole (ER)
1.6.1984-2.6.1984	Passage to Plymouth
2.6.1984-16.11.1984	Plymouth (rlvg ON.1028: 9/0)
16.11.1984-17.11.1984	Passage to Newhaven
17.11.1984-16.4.1985	Newhaven (rlvg ON.1045: 1/0)
16.4.1985-18.4.1985	Passage to St Helier
18.4.1985-22.9.1985	St Helier (rlvg ON.1034: 22/17)
22.9.1985-2.11.1985	Cantell's Bt Yd, Newhaven (S, ER)
2.11.1985-3.11.1985	Passage to Gorleston
3.11.1985-11.4.1986	Great Yarmouth & Gorleston (rlvg ON.1065: 4/2)
11.4.1986-12.4.1986	Passage to Teesmouth
12.4.1986-17.5.1986	Teesmouth (rlvg ON.1110: 1/0)
17.5.1986-19.5.1986	Passage to Sheerness
19.5.1986-12.12.1986	Denton Shiprepairers Ltd, Otterham Quay (std, ER)
12.12.1986-8.4.1987	Sheerness (rlvg ON.1027: 6/0)
9.4.1987-20.7.1987	Harwich (rlvg ON.1060: 4/2)
20.7.1987-20.3.1988	Great Yarmouth & Gorleston (rlvg ON.1065: 8/9)
20.3.1988-22.3.1988	Passage to South Shields
22.3.1988-11.6.1988	Robson's Bt Yd, South Shields (S)
11.6.1988-13.9.1988	Whitby (rlvg ON.1033: 10/7)
13.9.1988-1.10.1988	Leggett's Bt Yd, Grimsby (ER)
1.10.1988-2.10.1988	Passage to Rochester
2.10.1988-13.12.1988	Sheerness (rlvg ON.1027: 6/0)
13.12.1988-15.12.1988	Passage to Alderney
15.12.1988-3.2.1989	Alderney (rlvg ON.1045: 1/0)
3.2.1989-5.2.1989	Passage to Harwich
5.2.1989-30.4.1989	Harwich (rlvg ON.1060: 1/0)
30.4.1989-5.5.1989	Fletchers Bt Yd, Lowestoft (ER)
5.5.1989-17.7.1989	Great Yarmouth & Gorleston (rlvg ON.1065: 1/0)
17.7.1989-1.11.1989	Denton Shiprepairers Ltd, Otterham Quay (S)
1.11.1989-29.4.1990	Ramsgate (rlvg ON.1042: 8/1)
29.4.1990-29.6.1990	Harwich (rlvg ON.1060: 1/0)
29.6.1990-7.7.1990	Denton Shiprepairers Ltd, Otterham Quay (ER)
7.7.1990-22.10.1990	Great Yarmouth & Gorleston (rlvg ON.1065: 5/2)
22.10.1990-11.4.1991	Denton Shiprepairers Ltd, Otterham Quay (ER)
11.4.1991-28.6.1991	Sheerness (rlvg ON.1027: 7/4)
28.6.1991-14.9.1991	Harwich (rlvg ON.1060: 5/2)
14.9.1991-17.2.1992	Great Yarmouth & Gorleston (rlvg ON.1065: 6/0)
17.2.1992-30.4.1992	Denton Shiprepairers Ltd, Otterham Quay (S)
30.4.1992-16.10.1992	Sheerness (rlvg ON.1027: 27/0)
16.10.1992-20.10.1992	Denton Shiprepairers Ltd, Otterham Quay (ER)
20.10.1992-6.12.1992	Harwich (rlvg ON.1060: 2/0)
6.12.1992-8.2.1993	Denton Shiprepairers Ltd, Otterham Quay (std)
8.2.1993-13.2.1993	Sheerness (rlvg ON.1027)
13.2.1993-9.4.1993	Great Yarmouth & Gorleston (rlvg ON.1065: 2/0)
9.4.1993-11.4.1993	Passage to Newhaven
11.4.1993-4.7.1993	Cantell's Bt Yd, Newhaven (S)
4.7.1993-5.7.1993	Denton Shiprepairers Ltd, Otterham Quay
5.7.1993-7.7.1993	Passage to Otterham Quay
7.7.1993-19.10.1993	Denton Shiprepairers Ltd, Otterham

	Quay (std, ER)
19.10.1993-17.12.1993	Sheerness (rlvg ON.1027)
17.12.1993-7.1.1994	Denton Shiprepairers Ltd, Otterham Quay (ER)
7.1.1994-8.1.1994	Passage to Harwich
8.1.1994-18.3.1994	Harwich (rlvg ON.1060)
18.3.1994-3.4.1994	Fletchers Bt Yd, Lowestoft (R)
3.4.1994-17.6.1994	Great Yarmouth & Gorleston (rlvg ON.1065)
17.6.1994-4.7.1994	Lowestoft (rlvg ON.1142)
4.7.1994-6.7.1994	Fletchers Bt Yd, Lowestoft (std)
6.7.1994-7.7.1994	Passage, refuelling at Humber, to Tynemouth
7.7.1994-3.8.1994	Tynemouth (rlvg ON.1061)
3.8.1994-4.8.1994	Passage to Aberdeen
4.8.1994-12.8.1994	Aberdeen (rlvg ON.1050)
12.8.1994-14.8.1994	Passage (via Eyemouth 12.8.94 and Whitby 13.8.94)
14.8.1994-1.10.1994	Great Yarmouth & Gorleston (rlvg ON.1065)
1.10.1994-4.10.1994	Passage (via Sheerness)
4.10.1994-15.1.1995	Denton Shiprepairers Ltd, Otterham Quay (S)
15.1.1995-4.3.1995	Sheerness (rlvg ON.1027)
4.3.1995-11.5.1995	Harwich (rlvg ON.1060)
11.5.1995-1.8.1995	Great Yarmouth & Gorleston (rlvg ON.1065)
1.8.1995-7.8.1995	Lowestoft (rlvg ON.1132)
7.8.1995-13.8.1995	Fletchers Bt Yd, Lowestoft (R)
13.8.1995-16.8.1995	Sheerness (rlvg ON.1027)
16.8.1995-30.10.1995	Denton Shiprepairers Ltd, Otterham Quay (S)
30.10.1995-5.11.1995	Denton Shiprepairers Ltd, Otterham Quay (std)
5.11.1995-8.11.1995	Passage to Dunbar (via Sheerness 5.11.95, Lowestoft 6.11.95, Scarborough 7.11.95)
8.11.1995-24.11.1995	Dunbar (rlvg ON.1034)
24.11.1995-3.12.1995	Amble Marina, Amble (std)
3.12.1995-7.12.1995	Passage (via Bridlington 3.12.95, Lowestoft 4.12.95, Ramsgate 5.12.95, Newhaven 6.12.95)
7.12.1995-5.2.1996	RNLI Depot, Poole (Larne CT)
5.2.1996-7.2.1996	Passage (via Newhaven 5.2.96, Sheerness 6.2.95)
7.2.1996-21.5.1996	Denton Shiprepairers Ltd, Otterham Quay (R, std)
21.5.1996-24.5.1996	Passage to Alderney (via Sheerness 21.5.96, Ramsgate 22.5.96, Brighton 23.5.96)
24.5.1996-22.6.1996	Alderney (rlvg ON.1199)
22.6.1996-26.6.1996	RNLI Depot, Poole (std)
26.6.1996-28.6.1996	Passage to Gorleston (via Newhaven 26.6.96 and Ramsgate 27.6.96, passage to Gorleston as station relief while ON.1208 has a paint/tidy up before naming)
28.6.1996-20.7.1996	Great Yarmouth & Gorleston (rlvg ON.1208, which went to Littlehampton for engine repairs and paint up before naming ceremony)
20.7.1996-22.7.1996	Passage to Amble (via Lowestoft 20.7.96, Scarborough 21.7.96)
22.7.1996-24.7.1996	Amble (awaiting changeover)
24.7.1996-5.11.1996	Amble (rlvg ON.1004)
5.11.1996-7.5.1997	Hartlepool Marina (std)
7.5.1997-11.5.1997	Passage to Poole (via Scarborough 7.5.97, Gorleston 8.5.97, Ramsgate 9.5.97, Newhaven 10.5.97)
11.5.1997-20.5.1997	RNLI Depot, Poole (on sale list)
20.5.1997	RNLI Depot, Poole (T)

Notable rescues

During her time on station at Great Yarmouth and Gorleston, *Khami* was involved in a number of notable rescues for which her Coxswains and crews received formal recognition. The first of these services, on 9 November 1969, began at 7.55pm when *Khami* was launched under the command of Coxswain/Mechanic John Bryan to the Danish motor vessel *Karen Brayd* which had engine trouble.

In a westerly gale force 7 to 8 with a rough sea and rain squalls, the lifeboat made the rough passage of more than 8 miles to the Cross Sands light vessel and reached the

In order to accommodate *Khami* at Gorleston, this special mooring pen was constructed up river from the lifeboat houses, which had until then housed the lifeboat. (Grahame Farr)

As with all of the early 44ft Waveneys, *Khami's* superstructure was painted white during the first years of her service life. She is seen here in the river at Gorleston. (John Markham)

casualty at 9.35pm. In the intense cold and heavy breaking seas, Coxswain Bryan put the lifeboat alongside seven times to take off five crew members. She then stood by the vessel as its master made for Gorleston harbour, which was reached at about 3am the following morning. For this service the Bronze medal was awarded to Coxswain/Mechanic Bryan and the Thanks on Vellum accorded to the remainder of the crew.

In the early hours of 21 October 1973 *Khami* was launched under the command of Second Coxswain David Bennington after red flares had been sighted north of Gorleston harbour entrance. After a long search, the lifeboat found the converted naval pinnace *My Doris* listing heavily with two crew on board, in a north-west force 9 wind and very rough seas. Transferring the two people from the casualty would be too difficult, and so the lifeboat towed the casualty. At 6.30am, however, the casualty foundered and her two crew were in the water. Using the searchlight, the lifeboat was manoeuvred so that both survivors could be picked up at the first attempt. In the severe conditions the lifeboat touched bottom during the return passage but reached station safely. For this service the Thanks on Vellum was accorded to Acting Coxswain Bennington and Vellum service certificates were accorded to the remainder of her crew.

On 13 December 1974 *Khami* was launched to the 493-ton motor vessel *Biscaya* which had been in collision with a French tug. Under the command of Coxswain John Bryan, at 1.54am the lifeboat slipped her moorings and in a severe force 9 went to the vessel's assistance some 45 miles south-east of Gorleston. She arrived on the scene at 6.30am and found the ship listing slightly with her steering gear out of action. The lifeboat stood by to await a tug, which arrived at 10.34am, by when the casualty had begun to list severely.

Three of her crew took to a liferaft and were picked up immediately by the lifeboat. The other three crew remained onboard until 11.25am when the list increased. Coxswain Bryan then took the lifeboat close to the port bilge keel of the *Biscaya* and recovered the three men despite the heavy swell and the listing the casualty making the transfer very difficult. During the return passage the wind moderated to force 6, and Gorleston was reached at 6.25pm. For this service the Bronze second service clasp was awarded to Coxswain/Mechanic John Bryan, and medal service certificates were presented to the remainder of the crew.

On 22 December 1979 *Khami* was launched to the fishing vessel *St Margarite* which had sent out a Mayday. The lifeboat reached the vessel at 6.25pm on the Scroby Sand, and found her being washed by heavy breaking swell and sea. The wind was force 6 with a rough, steep sea, and approaching the casualty was difficult because the lifeboat was touching the bottom in the troughs. However, the lifeboat was successfully taken alongside long enough for the two men on board to be rescued, although the lifeboat hit the bottom in the process. Once the two men were on board, the lifeboat pulled clear of the bank and stood by the abandoned vessel. When the vessel bounced clear of the bank, at 7.15pm, the lifeboat went alongside and a tow line was fixed. The fishing vessel was then towed back to Gorleston, although she later sank at her moorings.

For this service, the Bronze medal was awarded to Coxswain/Mechanic Richard Hawkins, and medal service

certificates were presented to the remainder of the crew, Acting Second Coxswain Michael T Brown and crew members Stanley Woods, John Cooper and David Parr. The hull of *Khami* was undamaged during this service, despite the punishment it had taken on East Anglia's notorious sandbanks, testament to the strength and build quality of the Waveney.

Disposal

Khami was placed on the sale list on 11 May 1997 and sold on 21 May 1999 to the Royal Volunteer Coastal Patrol, Australia, for service in the Botany Bay Division, New South Wales, as a Coast Guard vessel and lifeboat. She was repainted in the livery of the Coastal Patrol (white hull) at Souter Shipyard, Cowes, IOW, and kept at the RNLI Depot, Poole, until being shipped out to Australia. She has been renamed *P&O Nedlloyd Stratheden*.

Above Stationed at Great Yarmouth and Gorleston, *Khami* arriving at Carrow Bridge, Norwich, with kidney patients stranded by the snow in February 1979. (Eastern Daily Press)

Below While in the Relief Fleet, *Khami* served at many stations and is seen here moored at Navyard Wharf while relieving at Harwich in May 1995. (Nicholas Leach)

Key information

Official Number	1003
Year built	1967
Builder	Brooke Marine, Lowestoft
Yard No.	B 350
Cost	£35,000
Weight	17t18

Donor

Provided by a gift from the Ancient Order of Foresters Friendly Society, the 8th boat donated by the Order in the 20th century, together with RNLI Funds.
Named on 26 July 1967 at Dover by HRH Princess Marina, Duchess of Kent.

Stations

Stations	Years on station	Record
Dover	26 Jul 1967 – 2 Oct 1979	202/140
Relief	7 Oct 1979 – 11 Jun 1984	49/18
Holyhead (TSD)	12 Jun 1984 – 14 Sep 1985	25/26
Relief	14 Sep 1985 – 27 Jun 1997	98/28

Movements

26.7.1967-7.8.1971	Dover (sl)
7.8.1971-31.8.1971	Brooke Marine, Lowestoft (rlvd by 44-001)
31.8.1971-1.2.1975	Dover (sl)
1.2.1975-31.5.1975	Brooke Marine, Lowestoft (rlvd by 44-001)
31.5.1975-3.6.1976	Dover (sl)
3.6.1976-24.10.1976	Brooke Marine, Lowestoft (rlvd by 44-001)
24.10.1976-2.10.1979	Dover (sl)
2.10.1979-7.11.1979	Dover (ER)
7.11.1979-10.11.1979	Passage to Cowes
10.11.1979-10.4.1981	Wm Osborne Ltd, Littlehampton (std)
10.4.1981-2.8.1981	St Helier (rlvg ON.1034: 4/0)
2.8.1981-3.8.1981	Passage to Harwich
3.8.1981-9.10.1981	Harwich (rlvg ON.1060: 1/0)
9.10.1981-10.10.1981	Passage to Gt Yarmouth
10.10.1981-19.1.1982	Gt Yarmouth & Gorleston (rlvg ON.1065: 3/0)
19.1.1982-1.2.1982	Denton Shiprepairers Ltd, Otterham Quay (std)
1.2.1982-28.3.1982	Sheerness (rlvg ON.1027: 1 launch)
28.3.1982-31.3.1982	Passage to Barry Dock
31.3.1982-2.11.1982	Barry Dock (rlvg ON.1018: 12/0)
2.11.1982-10.11.1982	Passage to Sheerness
10.11.1982-2.12.1982	Sheerness (rlvg ON.1027: 2/6)
2.12.1982-3.12.1982	Passage to St Helier
3.12.1982-13.1.1983	St Helier (rlvg ON.1034: 2/2)
13.1.1983-16.10.1983	Poole (rlvg ON.1029: 16/10)
16.10.1983-19.10.1983	RNLI Depot, Poole (ER)
19.10.1983-20.10.1983	Passage to Newhaven (passage service on 19.10.83)
20.10.1983-15.1.1984	Newhaven (std)
15.1.1984-3.5.1984	Newhaven (rlvg ON.1045: 5/0)
3.5.1984-11.6.1984	Denton Shiprepairers Ltd, Otterham Quay (S)
12.6.1984-14.9.1985	Holyhead (TSD: 25/26)
14.9.1985-30.9.1985	Holyhead (ER)
30.9.1985-3.10.1985	Passage to Mashford's Bt Yd, Plymouth
3.10.1985-1.4.1986	Mashford's Bt Yd, Plymouth (S, ER)
1.4.1986-19.5.1986	Plymouth (rlvg ON.1028: 4/3)
19.5.1986-12.8.1986	Mashford's Bt Yd, Plymouth (ER)
12.8.1986-14.8.1986	Passage to St Helier
14.8.1986-27.2.1987	St Helier (rlvg ON.1034: 6/0)
27.2.1987-1.3.1987	Passage to Mashfords
1.3.1987-1.6.1987	Mashford's Bt Yd, Plymouth (S, ER)
1.6.1987-1.11.1987	Plymouth (rlvg ON.1028: 8/0)
1.11.1987-2.11.1987	Passage to Alderney
2.11.1987-10.12.1987	Alderney (rlvg ON.1045: 2/0)
10.12.1987-4.2.1988	St Helier (rlvg ON.1034: 3/0)
4.2.1988-23.2.1988	Wm Osborne Ltd, Littlehampton (ER)
23.2.1988-24.2.1988	Passage to Ramsgate
24.2.1988-20.7.1988	Ramsgate (rlvg ON.1042: 10/1)
20.7.1988-21.7.1988	Passage to Weymouth
21.7.1988-27.7.1988	Weymouth (rlvg ON.1122: 0/0)

Faithful Forester with white superstructure and rather basic electronics configuration during her early years in service at Dover. (From a postcard supplied by David Gooch)

After problems with the mooring berth at Holyhead, *Faithful Forester* was temporarily placed at the station and kept alongside this pontoon, seen on 7 July 1984. (Tony Denton)

27.7.1988-28.1.1989	Mashford's Bt Yd, Plymouth (S)
28.1.1989-4.4.1989	Fowey (rlvg ON.1028: 2/0)
11.4.1989-4.5.1989	Alderney (rlvg ON.1045: 2/1)
4.5.1989-29.5.1989	St Helier (rlvg ON.1034: 2/0)
29.5.1989-4.4.1990	Mashford's Bt Yd, Plymouth (ER)
4.4.1990-12.7.1990	Fowey (rlvg ON.1028: 12/1)
12.7.1990-14.9.1990	Mashford's Bt Yd, Plymouth (S)
14.9.1990-15.9.1990	Passage to Alderney
15.9.1990-2.11.1990	Alderney (rlvg ON.1045: 2/6)
2.11.1990-8.12.1990	Mashford's Bt Yd, Plymouth (ER)
8.12.1990-18.12.1990	Fowey (rlvg ON.1028: 0/0)
18.12.1990-4.5.1991	Mashford's Bt Yd, Plymouth (ER, std)
4.5.1991-12.5.1991	Penlee (rlvg ON.1108 relief, which was rlvg ON.1085)
12.5.1991-26.7.1991	Fowey (rlvg ON.1028: 2/2)
26.7.1991-18.10.1991	Mashford's Bt Yd, Plymouth (S)
18.10.1991-8.12.1991	Alderney (rlvg ON.1045: 2/0)
8.12.1991-14.2.1992	Mashford's Bt Yd, Plymouth (ER)
14.2.1992-25.2.1992	Fowey (rlvg ON.1028)
25.2.1992-15.6.1992	Mashford's Bt Yd, Plymouth (ER)
15.6.1992-22.6.1992	St Helier (rlvg ON.1157)
22.6.1992-24.6.1992	RNLI Depot, Poole
24.6.1992-25.6.1992	Passage to Plymouth
25.6.1992-6.7.1992	Mashford's Bt Yd, Plymouth (ER)
6.7.1992-22.11.1992	Fowey (rlvg ON.1028: 6/6)
22.11.1992-25.11.1992	RNLI Depot, Poole (HC)
25.11.1992-24.1.1993	Alderney (rlvg ON.1045)
24.1.1993-11.3.1993	Mashford's Bt Yd, Plymouth (S)
11.3.1993-7.5.1993	Mashford's Bt Yd, Plymouth (std)
7.5.1993-15.5.1993	RNLI Depot, Poole
15.5.1993-31.5.1993	Fowey (rlvg ON.1028)
31.5.1993-19.6.1993	Mashford's Bt Yd, Plymouth (std)
19.6.1993-20.6.1993	Passage to RNLI Depot, Poole
20.6.1993-1.8.1993	RNLI Depot, Poole (Fowey CT)
1.8.1993-6.8.1993	Fowey (rlvg ON.1028)
6.8.1993-17.8.1993	Mashford's Bt Yd, Plymouth (std)
17.8.1993-18.8.1993	Passage to Dunmore East
18.8.1993-22.11.1993	Dunmore East (rlvg ON.1035)
22.11.1993-23.11.1993	Passage to Dun Laoghaire
23.11.1993-30.1.1994	Dun Laoghaire (rlvg ON.1036)
30.1.1994-24.3.1994	Arklow (rlvg ON.1029)
24.3.1994-13.6.1994	Dickies Bt Yd, Bangor (std as ER)
13.6.1994-16.6.1994	Passage to Courtmacsherry Harbour
16.6.1994-28.9.1994	Courtmacsherry Harbour (rlvg ON.1005)
28.9.1994-5.10.1994	Crosshaven Bt Yd (std)
5.10.1994-21.12.1994	Dunmore East (rlvg ON.1035)
21.12.1994-27.12.1994	Crosshaven Bt Yd (std as ER)
27.12.1994-8.1.1995	Dunmore East (rlvg ON.1035)
8.1.1995-9.1.1995	Passage to Dun Laoghaire (via Arklow)
9.1.1995-16.3.1995	Dun Laoghaire (rlvg ON.1036)
16.3.1995-20.3.1995	Passage to Fowey (via Arklow 16.3.95, Fishguard 17.3.95, Padstow 18.3.95, Newlyn 19.3.95)
20.3.1995-14.9.1995	Fowey (rlvg ON.1028)
14.9.1995-17.9.1995	Passage (via Padstow 14.9.95, Fishguard 15.9.95, Holyhead 16.9.95)
17.9.1995-25.9.1995	Port Dinorwic (awaiting collection)
25.9.1995-28.1.1996	Dickies Bt Yd, Bangor (S)
28.1.1996-21.2.1996	Conwy Marina (std, ER)
21.2.1996-22.2.1996	Passage to Rosslare (via Holyhead)
22.2.1996-3.4.1996	Rosslare Harbour (rlvg ON.1092)
3.4.1996-8.6.1996	Dunmore East (rlvg ON.1035)
8.6.1996-19.7.1996	Marine Port Services, Pembroke Dock (std)
19.7.1996	Falmouth Bt Co, Falmouth (std)

Notable rescues

Two services performed by *Faithful Forester* when she was stationed at Dover resulted in awards for Coxswain and crew. The first took place on 1 December 1975 when the lifeboat was launched under the command of Coxswain Arthur Liddon to the 1199-ton coaster *Primrose*, of Cyprus, which was reported in difficulty 3 miles east of Dover breakwater. The lifeboat slipped her moorings at 10.37pm to help as tugs could not get out of the harbour due to the prevailing conditions.

The wind was force 10, creating appalling sea conditions at the entrance to the harbour. While clearing them, the lifeboat was laid over on her beam ends but righted herself and carried on through the heavy seas. With the assistance of the ferries *Free Enterprise VII* and *Free Enterprise VIII*, at 11.30pm the lifeboat arrived at the casualty which was less than 1.5 miles off the Goodwin Sands. *Faithful Forester* had covered the 5 miles from Dover Harbour at an average speed of 7.69 knots despite mountainous seas reported to be in excess of 25 feet in height.

Once on scene, the lifeboat stood by the casualty, which was shipping heavy seas continuously. At 12.49am, with a wind speed reading of 100mph recorded by *Free Enterprise VII*, the lifeboat was for the second time laid on to her beam ends by a combination of sea and wind pressure. It was about a minute before the wind slackened and *Faithful Forester* righted herself.

The *Primrose* had rigged makeshift steering gear and was able to make slow headway despite the appalling conditions. On the advice of Coxswain Liddon, the casualty had gained some shelter from the lee of the land and was closer to Dover harbour. When two miles off the harbour, the *Primrose's* master requested a pilot to take her in. However, as the pilot vessel could not leave the harbour in the conditions, the lifeboat took station ahead of the coaster and led her to a berth. By passing alterations of course and speed, at 4.12am the *Primrose* had been safely piloted into Dover harbour.

Faithful Forester returned to her berth in the submarine pens at 5am. As a result of this fine seamanship exhibited by Coxswain Liddon, he was awarded the Silver medal. The Bronze medal was awarded to Second Coxswain/Assistant Mechanic Anthony Hawkins and the Thanks on Vellum was accorded to the remainder of her crew, Second Assistant Mechanic Richard Hawkins and crew members John Smith and Gordon David. These lifeboatmen had risked their lives to go out in a relatively small boat for some eight hours in the worst of conditions to assist the coaster.

The second notable service performed by *Faithful Forester* while stationed at Dover took place on 7 December 1977. The trawler *St Patrick*, of Lowestoft, reported a fire in her engine room when five miles south-east of Dover harbour. *Faithful Forester* was launched under the command of Coxswain Arthur Liddon at 6.27pm into a strong force 6 breeze, with a rough sea and poor visibility.

Once alongside the fishing boat, Second Coxswain Anthony Hawkins was put on board to help fight the fire and attend to the chief engineer who was suffering from burns, shock and smoke inhalation. While Second Coxswain Hawkins was on board, the lifeboat was manoeuvred alongside seven times, during which five crew members were taken off. Some damage was sustained by the lifeboat when the vessels rolled together due to the wind which had increased to gale force 8.

The ferry *Earl Leofric* was acting as on-scene commander. As a doctor was needed, a request was put out over the *Earl Leofric's* public address system for any doctor on board to come to the bridge. Dr Sotiris Mantoudis reported to the master, and was transferred to the fishing vessel by lifeboat. The operation to take him off the ferry and onto the fishing vessel was a difficult and dangerous one, as he descended over the ship's side on a boarding ladder, and it took three attempts before he could be got onto the rolling deck of the lifeboat.

Once the medical supplies and the doctor had been transferred to the casualty, the lifeboat landed the casualties at Dover and then returned to stand by the stricken trawler. Dr Mantoudis examined the chief engineer, while Second Coxswain Hawkins ascertained that the fire was under control. The local tug *Dominant* towed *St Patrick* into Dover harbour, which she entered at 8.55pm, and with the assistance of the lifeboat crew was secured alongside.

For this service a Doctor's vellum was awarded to Dr Mantoudis, a consultant surgeon at the University of Athens, for his help. The Thanks on Vellum was accorded to Coxswain Liddon and Second Coxswain Hawkins; Vellum service certificates were presented to the remainder of the crew, Second Assistant Mechanic John Smith and crew members Mark Smith, Roy Couzens and Robert Bruce.

While in the Relief Fleet, *Faithful Forester* served at many stations. When on relief duty at St Helier in 1982 a third notable service was performed. She was launched on 14 December at 1.56pm to the yacht *Festina Lent*, of Norway, under the command of Coxswain Michael Berry. The yacht's engine and steering gear had failed a mile south of St Helier harbour entrance. In force 5 to 6 winds, the lifeboat encountered moderate to rough seas as she made her way out of the harbour and found the casualty very quickly.

The yacht had been swept into an isolated outcrop of rocks. Despite having her anchor out, she was fast on jagged rocks. Without hesitation Coxswain Berry took the lifeboat into the area of heavily broken water. There was no hope of towing the yacht to safety, so swinging the lifeboat's starboard side to the yacht, he told her two crew to leap on board. He then executed a skilful withdrawal, stern first as there was not enough room to turn the lifeboat round. The rescue had taken only five minutes, and by 2.22pm the survivors had been landed at the harbour.

For this rescue, the Bronze medal was awarded to Coxswain Berry. Medal service certificates were presented to the remainder of the crew, Acting Second Coxswain David Aubert, Mechanic Dennis Aubert, Emergency Mechanic David Mills, William Hibbs and John Gray.

Disposal

Faithful Forester was placed on the sale list on 3 May 1997 and sold on 21 May 1999 to the Royal Volunteer Coastal Patrol, Australia, for service in the Narooma Division as a CG vessel and lifeboat. Repainted in Coastal Patrol livery (white hull) at Souter Shipyard, Cowes, she was kept at RNLI Depot, Poole, until being shipped to Australia. She arrived in Australia on 10 November 1999 and was renamed *P&O Nedlloyd Strathmore*.

Left After being stationed at Dover, *Faithful Forester* served for almost two decades in the Relief Fleet. She is seen here on relief at Dunmore East in April 1997. (Nicholas Leach)

Below After repainting in the colours of the Australian Coastal Patrol, *Faithful Forester* is lifted into the water at Souter's Shipyard, Cowes. (Peter Edey)

Key information

Official Number	1004
Year built	1967
Builder	Brooke Marine, Lowestoft
Yard No.	B 351
Cost	£37,838
Weight	17t13

Donor

An anonymous gift to record the friendship of William H Cavenaugh, Hazel M Dugan, Theodore L and Margaret N Harley with the donor.
Named on 27 September 1967 at Trinity House Pier, Harwich, by Captain G E Barnard, deputy master of Trinity House.

Stations

	Years on station	Record
Harwich	27 Sep 1967 – Mar 1980	173/77
Relief	1980 – 1986	49/14
Amble	9 June 1986 – July 1999	166/6

Movements

1.1.1968-1.10.1977	Harwich (sl)
1.10.1977-15.1.1978	Brown's Bt Yd, Rowhedge (S, rlvd by 44-001
15.1.1978-17.3.1980	Harwich (sl)
18.3.1980-24.3.1980	Passage to Crosshaven
24.3.1980-19.4.1980	Crosshaven Bt Yd (S)
20.4.1980-25.9.1980	Dun Laoghaire (rlvg ON.1001: 8/0)
25.9.1980-31.1.1981	Dunmore East (rlvg ON.1035: 1/0)
31.1.1981-6.2.1981	Tyrells Bt Yd, Arklow (ER)
6.2.1981-7.2.1981	Passage to Donaghadee
7.2.1981-7.5.1981	Donaghadee (rlvg ON.1005)
7.5.1981-8.5.1981	Passage to Beaumaris
8.5.1981-13.5.1981	Anglesey Bt Yd, Beaumaris (M)
13.5.1981-22.5.1981	Passage to Cowes
22.5.1981-2.8.1982	FBM Marine Ltd, Cowes (S)
2.8.1982-3.8.1982	RNLI Depot, Poole (T)
3.8.1982-11.8.1982	Torbay (T, R)
11.8.1982-13.8.1982	Falmouth (T)
13.8.1982-14.8.1982	Torbay (T)
14.8.1982-17.8.1982	RNLI Depot, Poole
17.8.1982-20.8.1982	Passage to Dun Laoghaire
20.8.1982-21.10.1983	Dun Laoghaire (rlvg ON.1001: 17/9)
2.2.1984-16.1.1985	Dunmore East (rlvg ON.1035: 10/4)
9.3.1985-22.5.1985	Donaghadee (rlvg ON.1005: 4/1)
22.5.1985-5.10.1985	Relief fleet
22.5.1985-5.10.1985	Fleetwood (rlvg ON.1036: 1/0)
5.10.1985-4.2.1986	Troon (rlvg ON.1029)
4.2.1986-9.4.1986	Rosyth Royal Dockyard (S)
9.4.1986-20.5.1986	Passage to Poole
20.5.1986-27.5.1986	RNLI Depot, Poole (allocated to Amble)
27.5.1986-30.5.1986	
30.5.1986-3.6.1986	Passage to Amble
3.6.1986-26.6.1989	Amble (sl)

During her service at Harwich, *Margaret Graham* was usually kept at these moorings in The Pound, near Halfpenny Pier, seen here on 19 June 1968. (Grahame Farr)

26.6.1989-14.7.1989	Amble Bt Co, Amble (S, rlvd by ON.1043)
14.7.1989-5.7.1990	Amble (sl)
5.7.1990-10.10.1990	Amble Bt Co, Amble (S, rlvd by ON.1034)
10.10.1990-10.10.1991	Amble (sl)
10.10.1991-13.12.1991	Amble Bt Co, Amble (S, rlvd by ON.1001)
13.12.1991-13.11.1992	Amble (sl)
13.11.1992-21.12.1992	Amble Bt Co, Amble (rlvd by ON.1001)
21.12.1992-27.1.1994	Amble (sl)
27.1.1994-15.4.1994	Amble Bt Co, Amble (rlvd by ON.1001)
15.4.1994-24.3.1995	Amble (sl)
24.3.1995-27.5.1995	Amble Bt Co, Amble (S)
27.5.1995-24.7.1996	Amble (sl)
24.7.1996-1.11.1996	Amble Bt Co, Amble (S)
1.11.1996-22.7.1999	Amble (sl)
22.7.1999-24.7.1999	Amble (std; the last Waveney to be stood down from station duty; ON.1176 placed on service at Amble at 8.15pm on 22.7.1999)
24.7.1999-30.7.1999	Blyth (std, after handover at Amble)
30.7.1999-23.8.1999	Amble Bt Co, Amble (numbers painted out for new owner)
23.8.1999	Whitby (taken over by new owner)

Disposal

Margaret Graham was the last Waveney in service with the RNLI. She was replaced at Amble on 22 July 1999, placed on the sale list on 30 July 1999 and sold out of service on 4 August 1999 to Scarborough Borough Council. Renamed *St Hilda of Whitby*, she is used as a pilot boat at Whitby.

Top　*Margaret Graham* in the early years of her service life, with her superstructure painted white. (RNLI)

Upper middle　At the mouth of Amble harbour in March 1999, *Margaret Graham* sets out to attend the Naming Ceremony of the new inshore lifeboat at Craster. (Nicholas Leach)

Lower middle　Entering Amble harbour, *Margaret Graham* dressed overall on 8 July 1999, the day her replacement arrived at the station. (Steve Dutton)

Bottom　*Margaret Graham* was sold out of service to Scarborough Borough Council and renamed *St. Hilda of Whitby*. She was used as a pilot boat and is seen here at Whitby in October 1999, largely unaltered, shortly after leaving RNLI service. (Nicholas Leach)

Key information

Official Number	1005
Year built	1968
Builder	Brooke Marine, Lowestoft
Yard No.	B 352
Cost	£35,000
Weight	17t5

Donor

Legacy of Mrs B A L Harris, London W1.
Named on 2 May 1970 at Barry Dock by Lady Traherne, wife of the Lord Lieutenant of Glamorganshire.

Stations

Stations	Years on station	Record
Barry Dock	14 Mar 1968 – 1974	109/44
Relief	1974 – 1979	33/7
Donaghadee	23 Aug 1979 – Dec 1986	8/43
Relief	1986 – 1993	56/18
Courtmacsherry Hbr	May 1993 – Sept 1995	17/7
Relief	1995 – 1996	2/0

Movements

13.3.1968-1.7.1969	Barry Dock (evaluation for one year; ON.806 also at the station for part of the evaluation period; on 1.7.1969 became sl at Barry Dock officially. On evaluation: 28/8)
1.7.1969-19.9.1969	Barry Dock (sl)
19.9.1969-8.11.1969	Ocean Fleet's Bt Yd, Birkenhead (S, rlvd by 44-001)
8.11.1969-2.11.1972	Barry Dock (sl)
2.11.1972-3.1.1973	Ocean Fleet's Bt Yd, Birkenhead (S, rlvd by 44-001)
3.1.1973-7.6.1974	Barry Dock (sl)
7.6.1974-8.6.1974	Passage to Birkenhead
8.6.1974-19.9.1974	Ocean Fleet's Bt Yd, Birkenhead (ER)
19.9.1974-21.4.1975	Dun Laoghaire (rlvg ON.1001: 2/1)
21.4.1975-25.8.1975	Tyrells Bt Yd, Arklow (ER)
25.8.1975-14.5.1976	Barry Dock (rlvg ON.1018: 15/0)
14.5.1976-24.7.1976	Dun Laoghaire (rlvg ON.1001: 4/0)
24.7.1976-20.12.1976	Dunmore East (rlvg ON.1035: 3/6)
20.12.1976-22.12.1976	Passage to Troon
22.12.1976-12.3.1977	Troon (rlvg ON.1006: 2/0)
12.3.1977-13.3.1977	Passage to Fleetwood
13.3.1977-22.7.1977	Fleetwood (rlvg ON.1036: 2/1)
22.7.1977-23.7.1977	Passage to Mashfords, Plymouth
23.7.1977-1.10.1977	Mashford's Bt Yd, Plymouth (S)
1.10.1977-22.4.1978	Barry Dock (rlvg ON.1018: 4/0)
22.4.1978-25.5.1978	Plymouth (rlvg ON.1028: 2/0)
1.6.1978-20.7.1979	Ocean Fleet's Bt Yd, Birkenhead (S, allocated to Donaghadee)
20.7.1979-27.7.1979	Trials
27.7.1979-1.8.1979	Donaghadee (T)
1.8.1979-25.9.1980	Donaghadee (TSD)
25.9.1980-2.5.1981	Tyrells Bt Yd, Arklow (rlvd by ON.1004)
2.5.1981-2.12.1982	Donaghadee (TSD)
2.12.1982-17.4.1983	Tyrells Bt Yd, Arklow (rlvd by ON.1002)
17.4.1983-1.3.1985	Donaghadee (TSD)
1.3.1985-22.5.1985	Tyrells Bt Yd, Arklow (S, rlvd by ON.1004)
22.5.1985-7.12.1985	Donaghadee (TSD)
7.12.1985-9.12.1985	Tyrells Bt Yd, Arklow (std)
9.12.1985-13.5.1986	Dun Laoghaire (rlvg ON.1001: 2/1)
13.5.1986-14.5.1986	Passage to Dunmore East
14.5.1986-19.10.1986	Dunmore East (rlvg ON.1035: 3/5)
19.10.1986-26.7.1987	Tyrells Bt Yd, Arklow (ER)
26.7.1987-21.12.1987	Fleetwood (rlvg ON.1036: 9/3)
21.12.1987-22.12.1987	Passage to Dun Laoghaire
22.12.1987-9.5.1988	Dun Laoghaire (rlvg ON.1001: 3/0)
9.5.1988-6.9.1988	Dunmore East (rlvg ON.1035: 8/8)
6.9.1988-10.9.1988	Dun Laoghaire (rlvg ON.1001: 0/0)
10.9.1988-19.1.1989	Tyrells Bt Yd, Arklow (S, ER)
19.1.1989-17.3.1989	Arklow (rlvg ON.1006: 2/0)
17.3.1989-27.5.1989	Dun Laoghaire (rlvg ON.1001: 0/0)
27.5.1989-1.11.1989	Tyrells Bt Yd, Arklow (ER)
1.11.1989-20.1.1990	Dunmore East (rlvg ON.1035: 3/0)
20.1.1990-18.9.1990	Tyrells Bt Yd, Arklow (std, ER)
18.9.1990-20.9.1990	Arklow (TSD)
20.9.1990-21.9.1990	Tyrells Bt Yd, Arklow (ER)
21.9.1990-26.10.1990	Howth (rlvg ON.1113: 1/0)

Arthur and Blanche Harris during her formal Naming Ceremony at Barry Dock on 2 May 1970. (Jeff Morris)

Flying the RNLI flag, *Arthur and Blanche Harris* puts to sea following her Naming Ceremony at Barry Dock. (Jeff Morris)

At moorings in the tidal entrance basin in the outer dock, *Arthur and Blanche Harris* seen at Barry Dock in October 1968. She was the first lifeboat to be kept afloat at the station. (Grahame Farr)

26.10.1990-16.12.1990	Tyrells Bt Yd, Arklow (ER)
16.12.1990-16.4.1991	Dunmore East (rlvg ON.1035: 3/0)
16.4.1991-17.4.1991	Passage to Dun Laoghaire (via Rosslare)
17.4.1991-2.7.1991	Dun Laoghaire (rlvg ON.1036: 5/0)
2.7.1991-17.7.1991	Tyrells Bt Yd, Arklow (R)
17.7.1991-10.10.1991	Arklow (rlvg ON.1029: 2/1)
10.10.1991-30.4.1992	Tyrells Bt Yd, Arklow (S)
30.4.1992-24.8.1992	Dunmore East (rlvg ON.1035:10/0)
24.8.1992-25.8.1992	Passage to Dun Laoghaire
25.8.1992-4.11.1992	Dun Laoghaire (rlvg ON.1036: 3/0)
4.11.1992-6.11.1992	Tyrells Bt Yd, Arklow (ER)
6.11.1992-12.1.1993	Arklow (rlvg ON.1029)
12.1.1993-1.5.1993	Tyrells Bt Yd, Arklow (S, ER)
1.5.1993-5.5.1993	Passage to RNLI Depot, Poole (via Angle, Falmouth and Newlyn)
5.5.1993-14.5.1993	RNLI Depot, Poole (CT)
14.5.1993-19.5.1993	Passage to Courtmacsherry (via Angle 16-17.5.93)
19.5.1993-28.5.1993	Courtmacsherry Harbour (CT)
28.5.1993-29.7.1993	Courtmacsherry Harbour (sl)
29.7.1993-29.7.1993	Crosshaven Bt Yd (HC)
29.7.1993-10.2.1994	Courtmacsherry Harbour (sl)
10.2.1994-10.2.1994	Crosshaven Bt Yd (HC)
10.2.1994-16.6.1994	Courtmacsherry Harbour (sl)
16.6.1994-17.6.1994	Passage to Valentia
17.6.1994-24.9.1994	Valentia Marine (S, rlvd by ON.1003)
24.9.1994-15.5.1995	Courtmacsherry Harbour (sl)
15.5.1995-15.5.1995	Crosshaven Bt Yd (HC)
15.5.1995-25.9.1995	Courtmacsherry Harbour (sl)
25.9.1995-19.1.1996	Crosshaven Bt Yd (std, ER)
19.1.1996-11.6.1996	Courtmacsherry Harbour (rlvg ON.1205)
11.6.1996-14.6.1996	Passage (via Newlyn 12.6.96, Salcombe 13.6.96)
14.6.1996-18.6.1999	RNLI Depot, Poole (std)
18.6.1999-22.7.1999	Souter Sh Yd, Cowes (painting)
22.7.1999-14.12.1999	RNLI Depot, Poole (std)
14.12.1999-20.12.1999	Passage to Tilbury (via Shoreham, Eastbourne, Ramsgate and Sheerness)
20.12.1999	Tilbury Docks (for shipping)

Notable rescue

The most notable rescue performed by *Arthur and Blanche Harris* took place on 14 September 1987 when she was on relief duty at Fleetwood. She was launched under the command of Coxswain William Fairclough at 8.50pm to the fishing vessel *Galilean*, of Penzance, which was taking in water 5 miles west of Blackpool Tower. In force 6 winds and rough seas, which were steadily worsening, the lifeboat was laid over on her beam ends on two occasions.

Once the lifeboat had reached the casualty, it was agreed that an attempt to tow would her be made to reduce the risks involved with taking the lifeboat alongside and transferring

the crew of the fishing vessel. A tow line was secured at the fourth attempt and at 10.20pm the tow got underway. For 2 hours the tow was maintained despite the heavy seas breaking over both lifeboat and casualty.

However, shortly after midnight the fishing vessel became unstable with a large amount of water in her hull. The crew therefore decided to abandon her and got into their liferaft. Once clear of the sinking vessel, the two men were taken onboard the lifeboat which stood by until the fishing vessel sank. The lifeboat then returned to Fleetwood at 1.10am on 15 September and the survivors were landed.

For this service, the Thanks on Vellum was accorded to Coxswain Fairclough, and Vellum service certificates were presented to the remainder of the crew.

Disposal

Arthur and Blanche Harris was placed on the sale list on 14 June 1996 and sold on 21 May 1999 to the Royal Volunteer Coastal Patrol, Australia, for service in the Ulladulla Division as a Coast Guard vessel and lifeboat. After being repainted in the Coastal Patrol colours (white hull) she was kept at the RNLI Depot, Poole, until being shipped out to Australia and renamed *P&O Nedlloyd Strathallan*.

Top   In the small picturesque harbour at Donaghadee, *Arthur and Blanche Harris* at moorings in April 1985. (Tony Moore)

Upper middle   On exercise with an Army helicopter in August 1985, *Arthur and Blanche Harris* during her time at Donaghadee, County Down, Northern Ireland. (Colin Watson)

Lower middle   *Arthur and Blanche Harris* moored at Courtmacsherry Harbour, August 1995. (Nicholas Leach)

Bottom   Awaiting disposal, *Arthur and Blanche Harris* at the RNLI Depot, Poole, in July 1996. (Nicholas Leach)

Key information

Official Number	1006
Year built	1968
Builder	Brooke Marine, Lowestoft
Yard No.	B 353
Cost	£34,386
Weight	17t18

Donor

Legacy of the late W A Cargill, Carruth, Bridge of Weir, in memory of his mother.
Named 5 August 1968 at Troon by Mrs Connel Leggatt.

Stations

	Years on station	Record
Troon	Aug 1968 – Aug 1985	45/66
Arklow	7 Mar 1986 – June 1990	29/19
Relief	1990 – 1997	33/3

Movements

8.1968-16.5.1971	Troon (sl)
16.5.1971-23.6.1971	Morris & Lorimer, Sandbank (rlvd by ON.814)
23.6.1971-19.4.1972	Troon (sl)
19.4.1972-22.5.1972	Morris & Lorimer, Sandbank (rlvd by ON.814)
22.5.1972-22.4.1976	Troon (sl)
22.4.1976-7.6.1976	Morris & Lorimer, Sandbank (rlvd by ON.813)
7.6.1976-20.2.1977	Troon (sl)
20.2.1977-12.3.1977	Morris & Lorimer, Sandbank (rlvd by ON.1005)
12.3.1977-5.2.1978	Troon (sl)
5.2.1978-22.4.1978	Morris & Lorimer, Sandbank (rlvd by ON.849)
22.4.1978-25.12.1978	Troon (sl)
25.12.1978-12.5.1979	Robertsons Bt Yd, Sandbank (R)
12.5.1979-1.6.1979	Troon (sl)
1.6.1979-7.9.1979	Robertsons Bt Yd, Sandbank (R, rlvd by ON.868)
7.9.1979-8.6.1981	Troon (sl)
8.6.1981-10.6.1981	Passage to Holyhead (rlvd by ON.1002)
10.6.1981-7.6.1982	Holyhead Bt Yd, Holyhead (S, RE)
7.6.1982-24.6.1982	Holyhead Bt Yd, Holyhead (T)
24.6.1982-24.9.1982	Holyhead Bt Yd, Holyhead (std)
24.9.1982-5.10.1982	Holyhead Bt Yd (40hr trials)
5.10.1982-7.10.1982	Passage to Troon
7.10.1982-12.11.1983	Troon (sl)
12.11.1983-18.2.1984	McAlisters Bt Yd, Dumbarton (S)
18.2.1984-26.8.1985	Troon (sl)
26.8.1985-28.8.1985	Passage to Arklow
28.8.1985-24.2.1986	Tyrells Bt Yd, Arklow (S)
24.2.1986-3.3.1986	Passage to Arklow
3.3.1986-19.1.1989	Arklow (sl)
19.1.1989-17.3.1989	Tyrells Bt Yd, Arklow (S, rlvd by ON.1005)
17.3.1989-16.6.1990	Arklow (sl)
16.6.1990-16.6.1990	Passage to yard (rlvd by ON.1029)
16.6.1990-8.1.1991	Dickies Bt Yd, Bangor (S, ER)
8.1.1991-14.1.1991	Passage to RNLI Depot, Poole (via Fishguard and Milford Haven)
14.1.1991-9.2.1991	RNLI Depot, Poole (Portree CT)
9.2.1991-16.2.1991	Passage to Portree (via Fowey 9.2.91, Padstow 10.2.91, Fishguard 11.2.91, Holyhead 12.2.91, Portpatrick 13.2.91, Oban 14.2.91, Mallaig 15.2.91, Portree 16.2.91)
16.2.1991-9.3.1991	Portree (CT)
9.3.1991-3.5.1991	Portree (rlvg ON.1042 TSD)

Arriving at Troon, *Connel Elizabeth Cargill*, with her superstructure painted white, approaches her berth. (From a photograph supplied by Ian Johnson)

3.5.1991-17.5.1991	Stornoway (ER, rlvg ON.1098)
17.5.1991-19.5.1991	Passage to Holyhead
19.5.1991-7.5.1993	Holyhead Bt Yd, Holyhead (S, ER)
7.5.1993-10.5.1993	Passage to Invergordon
10.5.1993-16.7.1993	Invergordon (rlvg ON.1033: 2/0)
16.7.1993-15.1.1994	Herd & Mackenzie, Buckie (std, R)
15.1.1994-22.1.1994	Invergordon (rlvg ON.1033)
22.1.1994-6.3.1994	Jones' Bt Yd, Buckie (std)
6.3.1994-9.3.1994	Passage to Portree
9.3.1994-27.5.1994	Portree (rlvg ON.1042)
27.5.1994-28.5.1994	Passage (via Lochinver)
28.5.1994-29.5.1994	Passage to Buckie
29.5.1994-8.6.1994	Herd & Mackenzie, Buckie (std)
8.6.1994-9.6.1994	Passage to Dunbar
9.6.1994-26.8.1994	Dunbar (rlvg ON.1034)
26.8.1994-27.8.1994	Passage to Invergordon
27.8.1994-27.8.1994	Passage (via Peterhead)
27.8.1994-28.10.1994	Invergordon (rlvg ON.1033)
28.10.1994-28.1.1995	Herd & Mackenzie, Buckie (S)
28.1.1995-29.1.1995	Passage (via Aberdeen)
29.1.1995-19.2.1995	Eyemouth (rlvg ON.1026)
19.2.1995-20.2.1995	Passage to Buckie (via Aberdeen)
20.2.1995-1.3.1995	Herd & Mackenzie, Buckie (std)
1.3.1995-4.3.1995	Passage to Portree (via Caledonian Canal 2.3.95, Tobermory 3.3.95)
4.3.1995-12.5.1995	Portree (rlvg ON.1042)
12.5.1995-14.5.1995	Passage to Buckie (via Corpach)
14.5.1995-8.7.1995	Jones' Bt Yd, Buckie (std, ER)
8.7.1995-9.7.1995	Passage to Dunbar (via Peterhead)
9.7.1995-2.10.1995	Dunbar (rlvg ON.1034)
2.10.1995-3.10.1995	Passage to Invergordon (via Peterhead)
3.10.1995-18.12.1995	Invergordon (rlvg ON.1033)
18.12.1995-6.7.1996	Buckie Bt Yd, Buckie (std, ER)
6.7.1996-7.7.1996	Passage to Blyth (via Montrose)
7.7.1996-11.7.1996	Blyth (rlvg ON.1204 prior to Naming Ceremony)
11.7.1996-13.8.1996	Blyth (rlvg ON.1204)
13.8.1996-26.9.1996	Whitby (rlvg ON.1212)
26.9.1996-27.9.1996	Passage to Buckie, (via Eyemouth)
27.9.1996-28.9.1996	Passage to Buckie (via Aberdeen)
28.9.1996-28.11.1996	Buckie Bt Yd, Buckie (std)
28.11.1996-29.11.1996	Passage to Dunbar (via Aberdeen; passage crew from Broughty Ferry)
29.11.1996-22.12.1996	Dunbar (rlvg ON.1207)
22.12.1996-23.12.1996	Dunbar (ER, awaiting passage to Eyemouth)
23.12.1996-10.1.1997	Coastal Marine, Eyemouth (R)

Top In her later years at Troon, *Connel Elizabeth Cargill* was painted in the standard orange livery. She is seen here approaching the harbour. (Ian Johnson)

Upper middle Seen in July 1984 shortly before being replaced by a 52ft Arun, *Connel Elizabeth Cargill* moored in the dock at Troon. (Tony Denton)

Lower middle Leaving Arklow, *Connel Elizabeth Cargill* sets out for a routine training exercise, March 1986. (Tony Moore)

Bottom After service at Arklow, *Connel Elizabeth Cargill* served as a Relief lifeboat for six years. She is seen here at Dunbar, at moorings off Torness Power Station, in July 1994. (Nicholas Leach)

10.1.1997-15.2.1997	Eyemouth (rlvg ON.1209)
15.2.1997-21.2.1997	Coastal Marine, Eyemouth (std)
21.2.1997-9.3.1997	Dunbar (rlvg ON.1207)
9.3.1997-15.3.1997	Dunbar (std)
15.3.1997-28.3.1997	Eyemouth (rlvg ON.1209)
28.3.1997-31.3.1997	Eyemouth (std)
31.3.1997-2.4.1997	Eyemouth (rlvg ON.1209)
2.4.1997-1.5.1997	Eyemouth (std)
1.5.1997-3.5.1997	Dunbar (rlvg ON.1207)
3.5.1997-31.5.1997	Coastal Marine, Eyemouth (std)
31.5.1997-5.6.1997	Montrose (rlvg ON.1152)
5.6.1997-9.7.1997	Montrose (std)
9.7.1997-11.7.1997	Montrose (rlvg ON.1152)
11.7.1997-21.7.1997	Montrose (std)
21.7.1997-15.9.1997	Buckie Bt Yd, Buckie (std)
15.9.1997-18.9.1997	Invergordon (rlvg ON.1206)
18.9.1997-20.9.1997	Buckie Bt Yd, Buckie
20.9.1997-21.9.1997	Passage to Dunbar (via Peterhead)
21.9.1997-26.9.1997	Dunbar (rlvg ON.1207)
26.9.1997-27.9.1997	Eyemouth (rlvg ON.1209)
27.9.1997-24.5.1998	Coastal Marine, Eyemouth (ER)
24.5.1998-28.5.1998	Passage to Poole (via Whitby 24.5.98, Grimsby 25.5.98, Lowestoft 26.5.98, Eastbourne 27.5.98)
28.5.1998-14.4.1999	RNLI Depot, Poole (on sale list)
14.4.1999-23.5.1999	Souter Sh Yd, Cowes (painting)
23.5.1999-25.5.1999	Passage to Tilbury (via Eastbourne 23.5.99 and Sheerness 24.5.99)
25.5.1999	Shipped from Tilbury (to Australia)

Notable rescue

On 12 September 1980, *Connel Elizabeth Cargill* was launched at 1.35pm under the command of Coxswain/Mechanic Ian Johnson in a westerly storm and very rough sea to the Dutch dredger *Holland I*. The dredger had been working off Irvine Harbour fairway beacon and was in danger of breaking her moorings in winds gusting to force 10. Waves up to 20ft high were sweeping across the dredger's main deck.

The lifeboat cleared the harbour entrance and ploughed through the confused seas for three miles to reach the casualty. Several times she was hit by huge waves that broke over her and at one point rolled so violently to starboard that the side of her wheelhouse was nearly in the water. Coxswain Johnson frequently had to alter course and speed in heavy beam seas.

Connel Elizabeth Cargill reached the dredger at 2.20pm just under a mile from Irvine Harbour Fairway Beacon and on the edge of the surf line with just one stern mooring holding her in place. Coxswain Johnson decided to take the lifeboat alongside the dredger's starboard side to get the crew off one at a time. The lifeboat was taken alongside five times to rescue the dredger's crew, one man safely being taken off each time. Each approach was very hazardous as the lifeboat could have been trapped by the dredger should the stern mooring line have broken. On the first approach the lifeboat was thrown heavily against the dredger, damaging the Waveney's starboard plating.

The return passage to the lifeboat station was difficult because of the rough sea conditions. The survivors were all in the lifeboat's fore cabin, and were tended by one of the lifeboatmen. Full power was required to drive through the heavy seas off the harbour entrance. Once safely through, the survivors were landed at the lifeboat station.

For this rescue, the Silver medal was awarded to Coxswain/Mechanic Ian Johnson in recognition of his courage, leadership and fine seamanship; medal service certificates were presented to the rest of the crew, Second Coxswain/Assistant Mechanic Thomas Devenny, Emergency Mechanics Peter McClure and David Seaward, and crew members Robert Hannah and Roy Trewern.

Disposal

Connel Elizabeth Cargill was placed on the sale list on 27 September 1997 and sold out of service on 21 May 1999 to the Royal Volunteer Coastal Patrol, Australia, for service in the Sydney Division as a Coast Guard vessel and Lifeboat. Repainted in the Coastal Patrol colours (white hull), she was shipped out from Tilbury to Australia and subsequently renamed *P&O Nedlloyd Rawalpindi*.

Above Serving in the Relief Fleet, *Connel Elizabeth Cargill* seen at Blyth in July 1996. (Nicholas Leach)

Below Without any markings and her hull painted grey, *Connel Elizabeth Cargill* in the western Solent on 14 April 1999 after being taken out of service. (Peter Edey)

Key information

Official Number	1026
Year built	1974
Builder	Groves & Guttridge Ltd, Cowes
Yard No.	G&G 658
Cost	£100,000
Weight	17t18

Donor

Civil Service Lifeboat Fund.
Named on 3 August 1974 at Eyemouth by Lady Seal, in memory of Sir Eric Seal KBE CB, a former Vice-President of the RNLI and Chairman of the Civil Service Lifeboat Fund.

Stations

	Years on station	Record
Eyemouth	7 Feb 1974 – Mar 1996	153/45

Movements

7.2.1974-9.7.1975	Eyemouth (sl)
9.7.1975-31.10.1975	Cardnell's Bt Yd, Maylandsea (S, rlvd by 44-001)
31.10.1975-8.1.1977	Eyemouth (sl)
8.1.1977-14.3.1977	Cardnell's Bt Yd, Maylandsea (rlvd by 44-001)
14.3.1977-21.4.1978	Eyemouth (sl)
21.4.1978-25.5.1978	Cardnell's Bt Yd, Maylandsea (rlvd by ON.910)
25.5.1978-17.7.1978	Eyemouth (sl)
17.7.1978-11.9.1978	Cardnell's Bt Yd, Maylandsea (S, rlvd by ON.910)
11.9.1978-22.3.1980	Eyemouth (sl)
22.3.1980-12.6.1980	Cardnell's Bt Yd, Maylandsea (rlvd by ON.962)
12.6.1980-23.4.1981	Eyemouth (sl)
23.4.1981-6.6.1981	Coastal Marine, Eyemouth (rlvd by ON.962)
6.6.1981-19.2.1983	Eyemouth (sl)
19.2.1983-24.6.1983	Coastal Marine, Eyemouth (rlvd by ON.1043)
24.6.1983-9.12.1984	Eyemouth (sl)
9.12.1984-9.3.1985	Coastal Marine, Eyemouth (rlvd by ON.1043)
9.3.1985-26.10.1988	Eyemouth (sl)
26.10.1988-1.12.1988	Coastal Marine, Eyemouth (rlvd by ON.1043)
1.12.1988-18.12.1988	Eyemouth (sl)
18.12.1988-29.4.1989	Amble Boat Company, Amble (rlvd by ON.1043)
29.4.1989-25.4.1990	Eyemouth (sl)
25.4.1990-6.10.1990	Coastal Marine, Eyemouth (rlvd by 44-001)
6.10.1990-11.11.1991	Eyemouth (sl)
11.11.1991-11.2.1992	Coastal Marine, Eyemouth (S, rlvd by ON.1034)
11.2.1992-8.2.1993	Eyemouth (sl)
8.2.1993-8.4.1993	Coastal Marine, Eyemouth (S, rlvd by ON.1001)
8.4.1993-18.4.1994	Eyemouth (sl)
18.4.1994-9.6.1994	Coastal Marine, Eyemouth (rlvd by ON.1001)
9.6.1994-30.1.1995	Eyemouth (sl)
30.1.1995-3.2.1995	Coastal Marine, Eyemouth (R, rlvd by ON.1006)
3.2.1995-27.6.1995	Eyemouth (sl)
27.6.1995-3.9.1995	Coastal Marine, Eyemouth (R)
3.9.1995-24.1.1996	Eyemouth (sl)
24.1.1996-2.2.1996	Coastal Marine, Eyemouth (R)
2.2.1996-31.3.1996	Eyemouth (sl)
31.3.1996-7.5.1996	Eyemouth (reallocated to relief fleet; ON.1209 on station)
7.5.1996-15.5.1996	Amble Marina, Amble (std)
15.5.1996-18.5.1996	Passage to RNLI Depot, Poole (via Gorleston 16.5.96, Ramsgate 17.5.96,

The berth at Gunsgreen Quay, Eyemouth, built in 1964 to enable the lifeboat to lie afloat. *Eric Seal (Civil Service No.36)* was kept here throughout her service life. (Nicholas Leach)

	Newhaven 18.5.96)
18.5.1996-18.6.1996	RNLI Depot, Poole (std)
18.6.1996-2.7.1996	RNLI Depot, Poole (T)
2.7.1996-5.7.1996	RNLI Depot, Poole (Training Centre Staff doing RYA Certificate)
5.7.1996	RNLI Depot, Poole (on sale list)

Notable rescue

Eric Seal (Civil Service No.8) was stationed at Eyemouth, on Scotland's Border coast, throughout her operational life. The narrow entrance to Eyemouth harbour could be difficult to negotiate and in severe weather conditions on 14 and 15 October 1992 it was closed to all shipping. However when the Tyne Pilot launch *Norman Forster* was reported to be broken down with three on board, assistance was required.

Despite the difficult conditions at the harbour entrance, *Eric Seal (Civil Service No.8)* was launched at 11.06am under the command of Coxswain John Johnston. With great skill and using his knowledge of the harbour entrance, the lifeboat was safely got out and taken into deep water. Twice she struck the bottom as heavy swell at the harbour entrance had built up. Once out of the harbour, heavy seas broke over her, but she reached the casualty at 11.38am.

Despite the reduced visibility caused by heavy sleet squalls, the lifeboat was taken close enough to the launch for a tow line to be passed, and once secured the launch was taken in tow. Returning to Eyemouth was impossible, and so Coxswain Johnston headed north. The lifeboat eventually arrived at Port Seaton, on the Firth of Forth, at 3.05pm where the casualty was safely berthed. The lifeboat was unable to get into Eyemouth harbour as conditions at the harbour entrance were so bad, but she arrived at Burnmouth, to the south, at 6.45pm.

For this service, the Thanks on Vellum was accorded to Coxswain John Johnston in recognition of his skill, courage and outstanding leadership. Vellum service certificates were presented to the remainder of the crew, Second Coxswain/ Mechanic James Tarvit, Acting Assistant Mechanic David Collin and crew members John Buchan, John Purves and Robert Aitchison.

Disposal

Eric Seal (Civil Service No.36) was placed on the sale list on 18 May 1996, sold out of service in April 2000 and shipped to Walvis Bay, Namibia, for use as a lifeboat.

Top　On trials, *Eric Seal (Civil Service No.36)* makes a fine site at speed. (RNLI)

Upper middle　Passing through the narrow harbour entrance at Eyemouth, *Eric Seal (Civil Service No.36)* puts out on exercise on 7 August 1993. (Brian Chandler)

Lower middle　Returning from service *Eric Seal (Civil Service No.36)* seen entering Eyemouth harbour on 24 July 1994. She launched following reports that climbers were stuck on rocks and damaged her propellers during the launch necessitating repairs at her station. The rocky coastline of the Borders can clearly be seen in the background. (Steve Dutton)

Bottom　The first lifeboat in Namibia, *Eric Seal (Civil Service No.36)* dressed overall. (Photo spplied by Jon Jones)

Key information

Official Number	1027
Year built	1974
Builder	Groves & Guttridge Ltd, Cowes
Yard No.	G&G 659
Cost	£100,000
Weight	17t12

Donor

Legacy of Mr James Bissell Turnbull, Ilfracombe; together with a special gift received from Medway Lions Club and proceeds of the Medway Lifeboat Appeal. Named on 18 May 1974 at Sheerness Docks by Mrs R D Leigh-Pemberton, wife of the vice Lord Lieut of Kent.

Stations

	Years on station	Record
Sheerness	4 Apr 1974 – Mar 1996	649/297
Achill	28 Aug 1996 – Jan 1998	9/0
Relief	Jan 1998 – Nov 1998	24/7

Movements

9.3.1974-4.4.1974	Sheerness (CT)
4.4.1974-31.5.1975	Sheerness (sl)
31.5.1975-30.6.1975	Fletchers Bt Yd, Lowestoft (rlvd by 44-001)
30.6.1975-24.10.1976	Sheerness (sl)
24.10.1976-18.11.1976	Fletcher's Bt Yd, Lowestoft (rlvd by 44-001)
18.11.1976-19.11.1976	Passage (engine trials)
19.11.1976-17.12.1976	Fletcher's Bt Yd, Lowestoft (rlvd by 44-001)
17.12.1976-24.1.1978	Sheerness (sl)
24.1.1978-31.3.1978	Brown's Bt Yd, Rowhedge (S, rlvd by 44-001)
1.4.1978-30.4.1979	Sheerness (sl)
30.4.1979-21.9.1979	Cardnell's Bt Yd, Maylandsea (S, rlvd by ON.849)
21.9.1979-10.9.1980	Sheerness (sl)
10.9.1980-26.2.1981	Brown's Bt Yd, Rowhedge (S, rlvd by ON.853)
26.2.1981-1.2.1982	Sheerness (sl)
1.2.1982-31.3.1982	Denton Shiprepairers, Otterham Quay (rlvd by ON.1003)
31.3.1982-24.6.1982	Sheerness (sl)
24.6.1982-29.10.1982	Brown's Bt Yd, Rowhedge (S, rlvd by 44-001 and ON.1003)
29.10.1982-10.11.1982	Sheerness (sl)
10.11.1982-2.12.1982	Denton Shiprepairers, Otterham Quay (rlvd by ON.1003)
2.12.1982-14.7.1984	Sheerness (sl)
14.12.1984-5.7.1985	Denton Shiprepairers, Otterham Quay (S, rlvd by 44-001)
5.7.1985-15.12.1986	Sheerness (sl)
15.12.1986-9.4.1987	Denton Shiprepairers, Otterham Quay (S, rlvd by ON.1002)
9.4.1987-6.10.1988	Sheerness (sl)
6.10.1988-10.12.1988	Denton Shiprepairers, Otterham Quay (S, rlvd by ON.1002)
10.12.1988-7.2.1990	Sheerness (sl)
7.2.1990-22.4.1990	Denton Shiprepairers, Otterham Quay (S, rlvd by 44-001)
22.4.1990-12.4.1991	Sheerness (sl)
12.4.1991-26.6.1991	Denton Shiprepairers, Otterham Quay (S, rlvd by ON.1002)

The scene at Sheerness Docks for the Naming Ceremony of *Helen Turnbull* on 18 May 1974. (Jeff Morris)

26.6.1991-6.12.1991	Sheerness (sl)
6.12.1991-15.1.1992	Denton Shiprepairers, Otterham Quay (R, rlvd by 44-001)
15.1.1992-30.4.1992	Sheerness (sl)
30.4.1992-15.10.1992	Denton Shiprepairers, Otterham Quay (S, rlvd by ON.1002)
15.10.1992-8.2.1993	Sheerness (sl)
8.2.1993-9.2.1993	Denton Shiprepairers, Otterham Quay (R, rlvd by ON.1002)
9.2.1993-19.10.1993	Sheerness (sl)
19.10.1993-17.12.1993	Denton Shiprepairers, Otterham Quay (S, rlvd by ON.1002)
17.12.1993-16.1.1995	Sheerness (sl)
16.1.1995-3.3.1995	Denton Shiprepairers, Otterham Quay (S, rlvd by ON.1002)
3.3.1995-12.9.1995	Sheerness (sl)
12.9.1995-12.9.1995	Denton Shiprepairers, Otterham Quay (HC)
12.9.1995-18.3.1996	Sheerness (sl)
18.3.1996-9.5.1996	Denton Shiprepairers, Otterham Quay (S)
9.5.1996-14.5.1996	Sheerness (sl)
14.5.1996-15.5.1996	Passage to Poole (via Newhaven)
15.5.1996-29.6.1996	RNLI Depot, Poole (Achill CT)
29.6.1996-6.7.1996	Crew passage to Achill (via Torbay 29.6.96, Salcombe 30.6.96, Newlyn 1.7.96, Neyland Marina 2.7.96, Dunmore East 3.7.96, Castletownbere 4.7.96, Fenit 5.7.96, and Innisboffin 6.7.96)
6.7.1996-16.7.1996	Achill Island (CT)
16.7.1996-17.7.1996	Crew training (via Galway City)
17.7.1996-28.8.1996	Achill Island (CT)
28.8.1996-29.1.1997	Achill Island (TSD)
29.1.1997-31.1.1997	Kilrush Creek Marina, Kilrush (HC, R, rlvd by ON.1042)
31.1.1997-24.7.1997	Achill Island (TSD)
24.7.1997-26.7.1997	Passage to Bangor (via Ballyglass 24.7.97, Portrush 25.7.97)
26.7.1997-10.10.1997	Bangor NI (S, rlvd by ON.1042)
10.10.1997-18.10.1997	Bangor Marina (std)
18.10.1997-25.10.1997	Larne (rlvg ON.1079)
25.10.1997-11.12.1997	Malahide Boatyard (std, ER)
11.12.1997-14.11.1998	Fleetwood (rlvg ON.1156)
14.11.1998-21.11.1998	Fleetwood (std, awaiting passage)
21.11.1998-1.12.1998	Dickies Bt Yd, Bangor (for sale)
1.12.1998	Passage to Douglas IOM under new ownership

Notable rescues

While stationed at Sheerness, *Helen Turnbull* was involved in many outstanding rescues for which her Coxswain was formally recognised by the RNLI. The first of these award-winning services took place on 16 August 1975. After red flares had been sighted, *Helen Turnbull* was launched at 1.28am under the command of Coxswain/Mechanic Charles Bowry into a force 6 wind with rough, short seas. The casualty, the yacht *Eladnit*, was found at 2.10am but getting alongside was difficult as the yacht was aground on a mud bank. The lifeboat was anchored nearby, and two crew members manned the small inflatable which was veered down to the casualty.

The two lifeboatmen got on board and found five people, three adults and two children. With the flood tide gaining in strength, the only option to save the five people was to tow the yacht off the bank. A heavy towline was secured, and at about 3.10am the yacht was towed clear by the lifeboat at half throttle on the engines. Once in deeper water, a lull in the wind allowed Coxswain Bowry to bring the lifeboat alongside the yacht and the five survivors were quickly transferred from the yacht. One of the lifeboatmen remained on board, and the yacht was safely brought in to Sheerness Great Basin at 5.47am. For this rescue, the Bronze medal was awarded to Coxswain Bowry; medal service certificates were presented to the remainder of the crew, Assistant Mechanic Roderick Underhill and crew members Malcolm Keen, Colin Washford, David Hargreaves and Barry Powell.

The next notable service performed by *Helen Turnbull* at Sheerness took place on 30 December 1978. She was launched at 9.06pm after a red flare had been sighted in Gillingham Reach. In a strong gale, force 9, with rough breaking seas and frequent heavy snow flurries, her crew, under Coxswain/Mechanic Charles Bowry, found the casualty, the cabin cruiser *Ma Jolie II*. The cabin cruiser had lost her propeller in the difficult conditions and her anchor was dragging.

To approach the casualty, the lifeboat was taken through yacht moorings which presented a major hazard as they could easily foul the propellers. The heavy snow was by now continuous, and spray was being driven between the casualty and the lifeboat. Three times the lifeboat was taken through the yacht moorings to get alongside the casualty, during which the cruiser's two occupants were rescued. The lifeboat was then able to rejoin the main channel and landed the two survivors at Gillingham Pier. For this service, the Bronze 2nd service clasp was awarded to Coxswain/ Mechanic Bowry; Medal service certificates were presented to the rest of the crew, Emergency Mechanic Grant Burnham, Colin Washford, Ian McCourt and Martin Oliver.

The outstanding rescue of *Helen Turnbull's* service at Sheerness took place in 1980. On the night of 19 March, she was launched to the radio ship *Mi Amigo* which was

Dressed overall, *Helen Turnbull* **at sea following her Naming Ceremony in May 1974. (Jeff Morris)**

dragging her anchors in Black Deep near the Long Sand Bank, 24 miles from the station, in a strong easterly force 9 gale and a very rough sea. During the passage to the casualty, the lifeboat had to reduce speed as she was shipping water and pounding heavily in the rough seas.

Once on the scene, the lifeboat was manoeuvred alongside *Mi Amigo* in confused seas, which caused the casualty to roll heavily. Getting the lifeboat alongside in between the extreme rise and fall of the sea was very hazardous as she was working in very shallow water. However, on thirteen occasions the lifeboat was taken alongside the casualty, into very shallow water. Many of the attempts had to be abandoned as the lifeboat was in danger of being landed on the casualty's deck.

During these approaches, the four crew were successfully taken off one by one. During one approach, the lifeboat was slammed against the side of the ship but luckily nobody on board was injured. Once the last of the crew had been taken on board, the lifeboat was taken clear and into deeper water. She then set course for Sheerness, arriving in the early hours of 20 March.

For this service, the Silver medal was awarded to Coxswain/Mechanic Charles Bowry; the Thanks on Vellum was accorded to the rest of the crew, Second Coxswain Arthur Lukey, Assistant Mechanic Roderick Underhill and crew members Malcolm Keen, Ian McCourt and William Edwards.

Disposal

Helen Turnbull was placed on the sale list on 28 November 1998 and sold out of service to Elan Investments, Douglas, IOM. Renamed *Badger,* she was converted into a pleasure boat at Ramsey, on the Isle of Man, and subsequently kept at moorings in the outer harbour at Port St Mary. She was substantially altered for leisure use; the wheelhouse was enlarged and enclosed, and the whole superstructure was painted white. In September 1999, she was moved to Coburg Marina, Liverpool, for the winter but returned to the Isle of Man in Spring 2000.

Top   Moorings for *Helen Turnbull* at Sheerness Docks, with the crew on board preparing for a routine exercise, in September 1993. (Nicholas Leach)

Upper middle   On relief duty at Fleetwood in February 1998, *Helen Turnbull* puts out on exercise. (Nicholas Leach)

Lower middle   A new lifeboat station at Achill Island, County Mayo, was established in 1996 and *Helen Turnbull* was the station's first lifeboat. She was kept at moorings in Achill Sound close to Kildavnet Pier. (Nicholas Leach)

Bottom   After service, *Helen Turnbull* was converted into a pleasure boat and operated from Port St Mary, Isle of Man. Renamed *Badger*, she is seen here leaving Peel in June 2000. (Phil Weeks)

Key information

Official Number	1028
Year built	1974
Builder	Groves & Guttridge Ltd, Cowes
Yard No.	G&G 660
Cost	£100,000
Weight	18t2

Donor

Legacy of the late Thomas Field, Liverpool.
Named 17 June 1975 at Mill Bay Docks, Plymouth, by
the Duchess of Kent.

Stations

Stations	Years on station	Record
Plymouth	22 May 1975 – Jan 1988	182/91
Fowey	26 Jan 1988 – 1996	169/35
Relief	1996 – 1997	4/0

Movements

17.5.1974-31.3.1975	Plymouth (sl)
19.7.1974-17.8.1974	International Lifeboat Exhibition, Plymouth (as part of the RNLI's 150th Anniversary Celebrations)
31.3.1975-3.6.1975	Mashford's Bt Yd, Plymouth (rlvd by ON.890)
3.6.1975-14.6.1976	Plymouth (sl)
14.6.1976-22.7.1976	Mashford's Bt Yd, Plymouth (rlvd by ON.819: 1/0)
22.7.1976-1.11.1976	Mashford's Bt Yd, Plymouth (rlvd by ON.847: 3/0)
1.11.1976-22.4.1978	Plymouth (sl)
22.4.1978-25.5.1978	Mashford's Bt Yd, Plymouth (S, rlvd by ON.1005)
25.5.1978-1.7.1981	Plymouth (sl)
1.7.1981-20.12.1981	Mashford's Bt Yd, Plymouth (rlvd by ON.928)
20.12.1981-2.6.1984	Plymouth (sl)
2.6.1984-15.11.1984	Mashford's Bt Yd, Plymouth (rlvd by ON.1002)
15.11.1984-1.4.1986	Plymouth (sl)
01.4.1986-19.5.1986	Mashford's Bt Yd, Plymouth (rlvd by ON.1003)
19.5.1986-31.5.1987	Plymouth (sl)
31.5.1987-1.11.1987	Mashford's Bt Yd, Plymouth (rlvd by ON.1003)
1.12.1987-10.12.1987	RNLI Depot, Poole (Fowey CT)
10.12.1987-13.12.1987	Passage to Fowey
13.12.1987-16.12.1987	Fowey (CT)
16.12.1987-1.2.1989	Fowey (sl)
1.2.1989-7.4.1989	Tom's Bt Yd, Polruan (S, rlvd by ON.1003)
7.4.1989-4.4.1990	Fowey (sl)
4.4.1990-8.7.1990	Tom's Bt Yd, Polruan (rlvd by ON.1003)
8.7.1990-7.12.1990	Fowey (sl)
7.12.1990-14.12.1990	Fowey (R at station, rlvd by ON.1003)
14.12.1990-18.12.1990	Mashford's Bt Yd, Plymouth (R)
18.12.1990-12.5.1991	Fowey (sl)
12.5.1991-23.7.1991	Mashford's Bt Yd, Plymouth (rlvd by ON.1003)
23.7.1991-25.7.1991	Passage to Fowey
25.7.1991-15.2.1992	Fowey (sl)
15.2.1992-22.2.1992	Mashford's Bt Yd, Plymouth (S, rlvd by ON.1003)
22.2.1992-7.7.1992	Fowey (sl)
7.7.1992-8.7.1992	Passage to Appledore
8.7.1992-20.11.1992	Appledore Bt Yd, Appledore (rlvd by ON.1003)
20.11.1992-21.11.1992	Passage to Fowey
21.11.1992-16.5.1993	Fowey (sl)
16.5.1993-26.5.1993	Falmouth Bt Co, Falmouth (S, rlvd by ON.1003)
26.5.1993-3.8.1993	Fowey (sl)
3.8.1993-5.8.1993	Mashford's Bt Yd, Plymouth (R, rlvd by ON.1003)
5.8.1993-17.11.1993	Fowey (sl)
17.11.1993-15.1.1994	Falmouth Bt Co, Falmouth (S, rlvd by 44-001)
15.1.1994-14.7.1994	Fowey (sl)
14.7.1994-14.7.1994	Falmouth Bt Co, Falmouth (HC)
14.7.1994-24.1.1995	Fowey (sl)

Arriving on station at Plymouth, *Thomas Forehead and Mary Rowse II* makes a fine sight as she cuts through the water. (From a photo in the author's collection)

24.1.1995-24.1.1995	Falmouth Bt Co, Falmouth (HC)
24.1.1995-30.3.1995	Fowey (sl)
30.3.1995-1.9.1995	Falmouth Bt Co, Falmouth (S)
1.9.1995-4.6.1996	Fowey (sl)
4.6.1996-4.6.1996	Tom's Bt Yd, Polruan (HC)
4.6.1996-26.10.1996	Fowey (sl)
26.10.1996-2.2.1997	Falmouth Bt Co (S, std)
2.2.1997-15.3.1997	AV Seaworks Ltd, Dartmouth (std, ER)
15.3.1997-27.3.1997	Fowey (rlvg ON.1222)
27.3.1997-5.4.1997	Fowey (awaiting passage to Dartmouth)
5.4.1997-16.11.1997	AV Seaworks Ltd, Dartmouth (std)
16.11.1997-17.11.1997	Passage to St Helier (via St Peter Port)
17.11.1997-26.11.1997	St Helier (rlvg ON.1157)
26.11.1997-27.11.1997	Passage to RNLI Depot, Poole (via Alderney)
27.11.1997-1.12.1997	RNLI Depot, Poole (std)
1.12.1997-3.12.1997	St Helier (rlvg ON.1097 relief)
3.12.1997	RNLI Depot, Poole
1999	Shipped to New Zealand

Notable rescues

On 15 February 1978, *Thomas Forehead and Mary Rowse II* was launched to the trawler *Ella Gerda*, of Teignmouth, which had three on board and was in difficulty 10 miles south west of Rame Head. Under Acting Coxswain Patrick Marshall, the lifeboat left Millbay Docks, Plymouth, at 10.50am in a force 6 wind. The weather gradually worsened and by the time the lifeboat had reached the casualty the wind was gale force 9, with driving rain.

The trawler had steamed towards Looe and anchored east of the harbour entrance to wait for the weather to improve so that it could enter. The lifeboat stood by the fishing vessel and also anchored off the entrance to the harbour. For several hours the lifeboat laid at anchor with the Acting Coxswain and Motor Mechanic Cyril Alcock taking turns at the helm in the poor visibility.

At 7.45pm the skipper of the fishing vessel reported that his anchor was dragging. When she ran aground on rocks under a sheer cliff face, the skipper requested the lifeboat come in and take off the crew. The sea was breaking over the nearby reef and the casualty, making the lifeboat's approach very hazardous. Acting Coxswain Marshall then took the lifeboat alongside the fishing vessel twice despite the violent seas and heavy snow, and two men were taken off the trawler. At one point during these manoeuvres, the lifeboat smashed down on the casualty, denting her bows but her watertight integrity remained.

As the lifeboat began a third approach it was reported that the skipper had been washed overboard. However, this was not the case as he radioed a message to say he was still on board and he thought his vessel would be washed clear of the rocks. The vessel was eventually washed off as the tide rose. After a further two hours moored off the harbour entrance, the casualty entered escorted by the lifeboat. For this rescue, Bronze medals were awarded to both Acting Coxswain Marshall and Mechanic Cyril Alcock. Medal service certificates were presented to crew members Michael Foster and Ivor Lovering.

A routine service for *Thomas Forehead and Mary Rowse II* as she tows a disabled catamaran into Plymouth. (From a photograph supplied by Paul Russell)

Seven years later, *Thomas Forehead and Mary Rowse II* was involved in another notable service, in which lifeboats from Falmouth and Penlee were also involved. On 15 February 1985 the French trawler *Saint Simson* was reported to be sinking 19 miles off Lizard Point. First the Falmouth lifeboat, then the Penlee lifeboat, went to her aid. The latter escorted her towards Plymouth and as the casualty approached Plymouth, *Thomas Forehead and Mary Rowse II* was launched on service under the command of Coxswain John Dare.

The wind was force 8 as the lifeboat left Plymouth Sound at about 7.30pm, and by 8.15pm she had reached the casualty, which was rolling heavily with seas breaking over her decks. Some seas were reaching 50 feet in height. As there was no salvage pump available, the skipper decided he and his crew should abandon the fishing vessel. They were requested by Coxswain Dare to get into a liferaft as this would make it easier to get to them. After several attempts the line thrown from the lifeboat to the liferaft was secured. Despite a huge sea breaking over the trawler and liferaft, the lifeboat was taken to the liferaft and the survivors were transferred into the well of the lifeboat.

During the return passage, with *Thomas Forehead and Mary Rowse II* at full speed, falling off a particularly large sea severely pounded the boat and the radar stopped working. However, the lifeboat was intact and she reached Plymouth safely, where the survivors were landed. For this rescue, the Thanks on Vellum was accorded to Coxswain Dare and Vellum service certificates presented to the remainder of the crew.

Disposal

Thomas Forehead and Mary Rowse II was placed on the sale list on 3 December 1997 and sold out of service in 1999 to the Royal New Zealand Coastguard Federation. Renamed *Westgate Rescue,* she was used as a Coast Guard vessel and lifeboat operating from New Plymouth, Taranaki.

Top At Fowey, *Thomas Forehead and Mary Rowse II* moored alongside the pontoon in the river. **(Phil Weeks)**

Upper middle Seen at Fowey, *Thomas Forehead and Mary Rowse II* at her moorings opposite Berrills Yard. **(Nicholas Leach)**

Lower middle Showing a good turn of speed, *Thomas Forehead and Mary Rowse II* at sea off Fowey. **(From a postcard in the author's collection)**

Bottom With a grey hull, *Thomas Forehead and Mary Rowse II* out of the water at RNLI Depot, Poole, awaiting disposal in September 1998. **(Nicholas Leach)**

Key information

Official Number	1029
Year built	1974
Builder	Groves & Guttridge Ltd, Cowes
Yard No.	G&G 661
Cost	£81,000
Weight	18t1

Donor

Gift of Mr W P Courtauld and the Mayor of Poole's Appeal.
Named on 7 May 1975 at Poole by Lady Rayner.

Stations

Stations	Years on station	Record
Poole	Nov 1974 – Oct 1983	106/32
Relief	Oct 1983 – 1985	8/5
Troon	25 Aug 1985 – Oct 1987	53/38
Relief	29 Oct 1987 – 5 Jun 1990	9/0
Arklow	5 June 1990 – Feb 1997	78/26
Stored at Poole	6 Apr 1997 – 10 May 1999	1/1

Movements

17.11.1974-20.6.1981	Poole (sl)
20.6.1981-21.6.1981	RNLI Depot, Poole
21.6.1981-11.1.1982	Branksea Marine, Wareham (S, rlvd by ON.853)
11.1.1982-24.1.1983	Poole (sl)
24.1.1983-1.11.1983	Groves & Guttridge (S, std)
1.11.1983-8.11.1983	Passage to Troon
8.11.1983-18.2.1984	Troon (rlvg ON.1006: 2/0)
19.2.1984-7.3.1984	McAllister's Bt Yd, Dumbarton (S, ER)
7.3.1984-10.3.1984	Passage to Barry Dock
10.3.1984-20.11.1984	Barry Dock (rlvg ON.1018: 5/5)
20.11.1984-7.12.1984	Passage to Dumbarton (weatherbound at Fishguard 21-24.11.1984, weatherbound at Holyhead 25.11-4.12.1984)
7.12.1984-23.8.1985	McAllister's Bt Yd, Dumbarton (S, ER)
23.8.1985-25.8.1985	Passage to Troon (service: 1/0)
25.8.1985-29.10.1987	Troon (TSD)
29.10.1987-31.10.1987	Passage to Plymouth
31.10.1987-26.1.1988	Plymouth (TSD: 1/0)
26.1.1988-4.2.1988	Plymouth
4.2.1988-29.2.1988	RNLI Depot, Poole (ER)
29.2.1988-4.3.1988	Passage to Bangor
4.3.1988-11.9.1988	Dickies Bt Yd, Bangor (S, ER)
11.9.1988-6.11.1988	Fleetwood (rlvg ON.1036: 3/0)
6.11.1988-15.7.1989	Dickies Bt Yd, Bangor (ER)
15.7.1989-22.7.1989	Porthdinllaen (rlvg ON.1120: 1/0)
22.7.1989-23.7.1989	Passage to Dunmore East
23.7.1989-6.11.1989	Dunmore East (rlvg ON.1035: 4/0)
6.11.1989-2.6.1990	Tyrells Bt Yd, Arklow (R)
2.6.1990-5.6.1990	Passage to Arklow
5.6.1990-18.9.1990	Arklow (TSD)
18.9.1990-20.9.1990	Tyrells Bt Yd, Arklow (R, rlvd by ON.1005)
20.9.1990-17.7.1991	Arklow (TSD)
17.7.1991-10.10.1991	Tyrells Bt Yd, Arklow (S, rlvd by ON.1005)
10.10.1991-6.11.1992	Arklow (TSD)
6.11.1992-12.1.1993	Tyrells Bt Yd, Arklow (S, rlvd by ON.1005)
12.1.1993-31.1.1994	Arklow (TSD)
31.1.1994-23.4.1994	Tyrells Bt Yd, Arklow (S, rlvd by ON.1003)
23.4.1994-15.9.1995	Arklow (TSD)
15.9.1995-1.12.1995	Tyrells Bt Yd, Arklow (S, rlvd by 44-001)
1.12.1995-19.2.1997	Arklow (TSD)

At the end of her Naming Ceremony in May 1975, *Augustine Courtauld* casts off her moorings with the invited guests on board. (Jeff Morris)

19.2.1997-3.3.1997	Arklow (reallocated to Relief Fleet)
3.3.1997-29.3.1997	Arklow (rlvg ON.1223)
29.3.1997-3.4.1997	Arklow (awaiting passage to Poole)
3.4.1997-6.4.1997	Passage to Poole (via Milford Haven Marina 3.4.97, Newlyn 4.4.97, Fowey 5.4.97, Torbay 6.4.97)
6.4.1997-10.5.1999	RNLI Depot, Poole (std: 1/1)
10.5.1999-1.6.1999	Souter Marine Ltd, Cowes (hull respray, painted in Australian rescue colours)
1.6.1999-3.6.1999	Passage to Tilbury Dock (via Newhaven 1.6.99 and Ramsgate 2.6.99)
3.6.1999	Tilbury Dock (for shipping to Australia)

Notable rescue

Augustine Courtauld performed more than 100 services while stationed at Poole, many of which were routine. Some, however, were more demanding, such as that performed on 8 January 1982. In blizzard conditions, with the wind blowing force 10 and an extremely rough sea, she was launched to the motor cruiser *Trois Lions*, which was in difficulty 12 miles south of Poole.

During the passage to the casualty, *Augustine Courtauld* encountered some heavy breaking seas in the Swash Channel. The casualty was found 5 miles south of Anvil Point, unsure of her position. To make for Weymouth or Poole was considered too dangerous, so the lifeboat escorted the cruiser to Yarmouth, Isle of Wight. With the assistance of the Yarmouth lifeboat, the cruiser was brought to safety. For this service, a Letter of Thanks was presented to Coxswain Frank Ide and the Poole crew.

Disposal

Augustine Courtauld was placed on the sale list on 10 May 1999 and sold out of service on 21 May 1999 to the Royal Volunteer Coastal Patrol, Australia. Renamed *P&O Nedlloyd Strathaird,* she entered service in the Broken Bay Division as a Coast Guard vessel and Lifeboat.

Top   **Augustine Courtauld on exercise while stationed at Poole. (John Buckby)**

Upper middle   **Seen in August 1980, *Augustine Courtauld* at her moorings in Lilliput Marina at Poole where was stationed between 1974 and 1983. (John Buckby)**

Lower middle   **Moored in the Dock at Arklow in August 1985, *Augustine Courtauld* was the second Waveney to serve at this station in County Wicklow. (Nicholas Leach)**

Bottom   **With many other Waveneys, *Augustine Courtauld* out of the water at RNLI Depot, Poole, awaiting disposal in July 1997. (Nicholas Leach)**

Key information

Official Number	1033
Year built	1974
Builder	Groves & Guttridge Ltd, Cowes
Yard No.	G&G 663
Cost	£79,018
Weight	19t2

Donor

Gift of Miss Gwynaeth Milburn, Harrogate.
Named on 21 May 1975 by Duchess of Kent, wife of the RNLI President.

Stations

	Years on station	Record
Whitby	24 Nov 1974 – Dec 1988	239/51
Invergordon	1 Apr 1989 – May 1996	66/10
Relief	May 1996 – 1999	1/0

Movements

24.11.1974-14.1.1976	Whitby (sl)
14.1.1976-2.6.1976	Amble Bt Co, Amble (rlvd by 44-001)
2.6.1976-21.9.1976	Whitby (sl)
21.9.1976-7.10.1976	Amble Bt Co, Amble (rlvd by ON.941)
7.10.1976-7.10.1977	Whitby (sl)
7.10.1977-1.12.1977	Amble Bt Co, Amble (rlvd by ON.910)
1.12.1977-29.1.1978	Whitby (sl)
29.1.1978-23.3.1978	Amble Bt Co, Amble (rlvd by ON.910)
23.3.1978-7.4.1979	Whitby (sl)
7.4.1979-28.6.1979	Amble Bt Co, Amble (rlvd by ON.962)
28.6.1979-16.6.1980	Whitby (sl)
16.6.1980-17.6.1980	Robson's Bt Yd, South Shields (I)
17.6.1980-24.6.1980	Whitby (sl)
24.6.1980-13.9.1980	Robson's Bt Yd, South Shields (rlvd by ON.962)
13.9.1980-10.8.1981	Whitby (sl)
10.8.1981-10.9.1981	Robson's Bt Yd, South Shields (rlvd by ON.962)
10.9.1981-25.6.1983	Whitby (sl)
25.6.1983-10.9.1983	Robson's Bt Yd, South Shields (rlvd by ON.1043)
10.9.1983-11.3.1985	Whitby (sl)
11.3.1985-18.7.1985	Robson's Bt Yd, South Shields (rlvd by ON.1043)
18.7.1985-20.9.1986	Whitby (sl)
20.9.1986-18.2.1987	Amble Bt Co, Amble (rlvd by ON.1043)
18.2.1987-12.6.1988	Whitby (sl)
12.6.1988-9.9.1988	Robson's Bt Yd, South Shields (rlvd by ON.1002)
9.9.1988-12.12.1988	Whitby (sl)
12.12.1988-13.12.1988	Whitby (ER)
13.12.1988-14.12.1988	Passage to Sheerness
14.12.1988-20.1.1989	Denton Shiprepairers Ltd, Otterham Quay (ER)
20.1.1989-24.1.1989	Passage to Buckie
24.1.1989-1.4.1989	Herd & Mackenzie, Buckie (S for new Invergordon)
1.4.1989-24.7.1990	Invergordon (TSD)
24.7.1990-15.11.1990	Herd & Mackenzie, Buckie (S, rlvd by ON.1001)
15.11.1990-22.2.1992	Invergordon (TSD)
22.2.1992-9.5.1992	Herd & Mackenzie, Buckie (S, rlvd by ON.1034)
9.5.1992-20.4.1993	Invergordon (TSD)
20.4.1993-23.4.1993	Herd & Mackenzie, Buckie (engine change)
23.4.1993-11.5.1993	Invergordon (TSD)
11.5.1993-16.7.1993	Herd & Mackenzie, Buckie (S, rlvd by ON.1006)
16.7.1993-15.1.1994	Invergordon (TSD)
15.1.1994-22.1.1994	Herd & Mackenzie, Buckie (R, rlvd by ON.1006)
22.1.1994-27.8.1994	Invergordon (TSD)
27.8.1994-27.10.1994	Herd & Mackenzie, Buckie (S)
27.10.1994-6.10.1995	Invergordon (TSD)
6.10.1995-7.10.1995	Passage to Amble
7.10.1995-15.12.1995	Amble Bt Co, Amble (S)
15.12.1995-16.12.1995	Passage (refuelled at Aberdeen)
16.12.1995-20.5.1996	Invergordon (TSD)

The White Rose of Yorkshire in the harbour at Whitby after her Naming Ceremony on 21 May 1975. (Jeff Morris)

Moored in the pen specially constructed for her, *The White Rose of Yorkshire* at Whitby in October 1980. (Paul Arro)

20.5.1996-10.1.1997	Buckie Bt Yd, Buckie (std)
10.1.1997-14.2.1997	Invergordon (rlvg ON.1206)
14.2.1997-26.2.1997	Buckie Bt Yd, Buckie (std)
26.2.1997-16.3.1997	Montrose (rlvg ON.1152)
16.3.1997-18.3.1997	Montrose (completed relief duty)
18.3.1997-22.3.1997	Montrose (rlvg ON.1152)
22.3.1997-8.8.1998	Buckie Bt Yd, Buckie (std, ER)
8.8.1998-19.8.1998	Passage to Poole (via Peterhead 9.8.98, Dunbar 15.8.98, Whitby 16.8.98, Grimsby 17.8.98, Lowestoft 18.8.98, Eastbourne 19.8.98)
19.8.1998-27.5.1999	RNLI Depot, Poole (on sale list)
27.5.1999-18.6.1999	Souter Sh Yd, Cowes (painting before sale)
18.6.1999-8.7.1999	RNLI Depot, Poole (std)
8.7.1999-14.8.1999	RNLI Depot, Poole (return from painting in new colours)
14.8.1999-16.8.1999	Passage to Gorleston (via Eastbourne 14.8.99 and Ramsgate 15.8.99)
16.8.1999	Gorleston (std, prior to shipping to new owner)

Notable rescue

On 9 April 1988 the 24ft yacht *Cymba* was swamped by heavy, breaking seas as she entered Whitby harbour. She was swept onto rocks to the west of the harbour. The Whitby inshore lifeboat D-260 *Gwynaeth* was launched followed, at 8.45am, by *The White Rose of Yorkshire* under the command of Coxswain Mechanic Peter Thomson. The ILB picked up a man from the water but was unable to approach the casualty as conditions were beyond its limits close to the shore, so the Waveney was taken in.

The *Cymba* was in danger of being driven onto the rocks, so *The White Rose of Yorkshire* was taken in stern first, keeping her head to sea and thus preventing her being driven onto the rocks by the seas. The lifeboat gradually drifted towards the casualty, but Coxswain/Mechanic Thomson had to go ahead on both engines each time a large wave swept over the lifeboat.

Despite being very close to the rocks in shallow water, and in danger of striking the bottom, the lifeboat was taken towards the yacht. The first two approaches had to be abandoned, but on the third attempt the lifeboat got close enough to the yacht for a line to be thrown to a man who was in the water astern of the yacht. He unclipped the safety line with which he was attached to the yacht, was hauled alongside the lifeboat, and pulled aboard into the lifeboat's well amidships.

The lifeboat was then taken out through the heavy breaking seas and entered the harbour at 9.04am. The survivor was landed and transferred to an ambulance to be taken to hospital. For this rescue, Coxswain/Mechanic Thomson was awarded the Bronze medal, as was ILB helmsman Nicholas Botham; medal service certificates were presented to the other lifeboatmen involved.

Disposal

The White Rose of Yorkshire was placed on the sale list on 19 August 1998 and sold out of service on 11 June 1999 to the Canadian Lifeboat Institution. She was repainted in the CLI's livery and took part in the lifeboat gathering for the RNLI 175th Anniversary, at Poole, on 22 and 23 June 1999, representing Canada. After being at Poole, she was taken to Gorleston where she was kept until being shipped via Sheerness. She went to Canada for service at Delta Station, Robert Banks, which is situated just south of Vancouver, British Columbia. Designated *1A.001,* she covers the Strait of Georgia to the south of Vancouver. The Canadian Lifeboat Institution is a voluntary organisation set up to promote water safety and preserve life and property on the territorial seas and inland waters of Canada. The organisation provides equipment and personnel for marine search and rescue services, complementing the search and rescue activities of the Canadian Coast Guard which is dependent on federal government support.

Below Stationed at Invergordon, *The White Rose of Yorkshire* seen here moored in the West Harbour, July 1995. (Nicholas Leach)

Bottom After being taken out of service, *The White Rose of Yorkshire* represented the Canadian Lifeboat Institution at the RNLI's 175th Anniversary Celebrations at Poole in June 1999. (Nicholas Leach)

Key information

Official Number	1034
Year built	1974
Builder	Groves & Guttridge Ltd, Cowes
Yard No.	G&G 664
Cost	£100,000
Weight	18t2

Donor

Proceeds of Jersey Lifeboat Appeal. Named after Coxswain Thomas James King who was awarded the Gold Medal for the rescue of the yacht *Maurice Georges* on 13 September 1949.
Named on 30 May 1975 at St Helier by HM Queen Elizabeth, The Queen Mother.

Stations

	Years on station	Record
St Helier	Feb 1975 – Dec 1989	288/155
Relief	1989 – 1993	20/11
Dunbar	1 Aug 1993 – Jan 1996	21/0
Relief	1996 – 1997	0/0

Movements

3.2.1975-10.4.1981	St Helier (sl)
10.4.1981-2.8.1981	Wm Osborne Ltd, Littlehampton (rlvd by ON.1003)
2.8.1981-4.12.1982	St Helier (sl)
4.12.1982-12.1.1983	Wm Osborne Ltd, Littlehampton (rlvd by ON.1003)
12.1.1983-10.9.1983	St Helier (sl)
10.9.1983-13.5.1984	FBM Marine Ltd. Cowes (rlvd by 1002)
13.5.1984-19.4.1985	St Helier (sl)
19.4.1985-20.4.1985	Passage to Newhaven
20.4.1985-5.9.1985	Cantell's Bt Yd, Newhaven (S, rlvd by ON.1002)
5.9.1985-21.9.1985	RNLI Depot, Poole (T)
21.9.1985-14.8.1986	St Helier (sl)
14.8.1986-27.2.1987	Wm Osborne Ltd, Littlehampton (rlvd by ON.1003)
27.2.1987-19.12.1987	St Helier (sl)
19.12.1987-4.2.1988	Wm Osborne Ltd, Littlehampton (rlvd by ON.1003)
4.2.1988-4.5.1989	St Helier (sl)
4.5.1989-24.5.1989	South Pier Bt Yd, St Helier (rlvd by ON.1003)
24.5.1989-30.12.1989	St Helier (sl, replaced by new lifeboat ON.1157 on 13.12.1989)
30.12.1989-30.12.1989	Passage to Poole
30.12.1989-3.1.1990	RNLI Depot, Poole (Depot relief)
3.1.1990-8.1.1990	Passage to Amble
8.1.1990-5.7.1990	Amble Boat Company Ltd (S)
5.7.1990-11.10.1990	Amble (rlvg ON.1004)
11.10.1990-14.12.1990	Blyth (rlvg ON.1079)
14.12.1990-10.1.1991	Amble Boat Company Ltd (ER)
10.1.1991-23.1.1991	Tynemouth (rlvg ON.1061)
23.1.1991-14.2.1991	Robson's Bt Yd South Shields (ER)
14.2.1991-15.2.1991	Passage to Buckie
15.2.1991-14.5.1991	Herd & Mackenzie, Buckie (ER)
14.5.1991-16.8.1991	Jones' Bt Yd, Buckie (S)
16.8.1991-18.8.1991	Passage to Portree (rlvg ON.1042)
18.8.1991-13.10.1991	Portree (rlvg ON.1042)
13.10.1991-16.10.1991	Passage to Buckie
16.10.1991-9.11.1991	Herd & Mackenzie, Buckie (ER)
9.11.1991-10.11.1991	Passage to Eyemouth
10.11.1991-15.2.1992	Eyemouth (rlvg ON.1026)
15.2.1992-16.2.1992	Passage to Buckie
16.2.1992-22.2.1992	Herd & Mackenzie, Buckie (R)
22.2.1992-9.5.1992	Invergordon (rlvg ON.1033: 2/2)
9.5.1992-14.1.1993	Herd & Mackenzie, Buckie (S, ER)
14.1.1993-19.1.1993	Passage to Portree (via Caledonian Canal, Fort Augustus, Fort William)
19.1.1993-25.3.1993	Portree (rlvg ON.1042)
25.3.1993-31.3.1993	Passage to Eyemouth (stormbound at Peterhead 28.3.1993)
31.3.1993-11.6.1993	Coastal Marine, Eyemouth (S)
11.6.1993-15.6.1993	Passage to Poole
15.6.1993-26.6.1993	RNLI Depot, Poole (Dunbar CT)
26.6.1993-30.6.1993	Passage (to Dunbar; overnight exercise at Newhaven 26-7.6.1993)
30.6.1993-24.7.1993	Dunbar (CT)

Named after one of the station's outstanding Coxswains, *Thomas James King* served at St Helier in the Channel Islands for over 14 years. (By courtesy of RNLI Jersey)

Passing through the narrow entrance to Dunbar harbour, *Thomas James King* makes a fine sight as she sets out on 17 July 1993 during the station's Lifeboat Day. (Steve Dutton)

24.7.1993-25.7.1993	Passage to Aberdeen and return to Dunbar
25.7.1993-1.8.1993	Dunbar (at station)
1.8.1993-20.1.1994	Dunbar (TSD)
20.1.1994-20.1.1994	Coastal Marine, Eyemouth (HC)
20.1.1994-2.3.1994	Dunbar (TSD)
2.3.1994-8.3.1994	Coastal Marine, Eyemouth (R; Dunbar without ALB)
8.3.1994-14.6.1994	Dunbar (sl)
14.6.1994-25.8.1994	Coastal Marine, Eyemouth (S)
25.8.1994-23.2.1995	Dunbar (sl)
23.2.1995-23.2.1995	Coastal Marine, Eyemouth (HC)
23.2.1995-11.7.1995	Dunbar (sl)
11.7.1995-29.9.1995	Amble Boat Company Ltd (S, rlvd by ON.1062)
29.9.1995-6.11.1995	Dunbar (sl)
6.11.1995-23.11.1995	Coastal Marine, Eyemouth (R, rlvd by ON.1002)
23.11.1995-19.12.1995	Dunbar (sl)
19.12.1995-22.1.1996	Buckie Bt Yd, Buckie (std, ER)
22.1.1996-23.1.1996	Passage to Eyemouth (via Aberdeen)
23.1.1996-24.1.1996	Eyemouth
24.1.1996-2.2.1996	Eyemouth (rlvg ON.1026)
2.2.1996-12.2.1996	Coastal Marine, Eyemouth (S, std)
12.2.1996-26.4.1996	Dunbar (rlvg ON.1207)
26.4.1996-5.6.1996	Coastal Marine, Eyemouth (R, std)
5.6.1996-9.6.1996	Passage to Buckie (via Dunbar 5.6.96 and Peterhead 8.6.96)
9.6.1996-24.7.1996	Buckie Bt Yd, Buckie (S, std)
24.7.1996-25.7.1996	Passage to Portree, via Scrabster
25.7.1996-16.8.1996	Portree (rlvg ON.1214)
16.8.1996-18.8.1996	Passage to Buckie Shipyards (via Corpach 16.8.99 and Fort Augustus 17.8.99)
18.8.1996-30.8.1996	Buckie Bt Yd, Buckie (std, ER)
30.8.1996-13.9.1996	Invergordon (rlvg ON.1206)
13.9.1996-8.10.1996	Buckie Bt Yd, Buckie (std)
8.10.1996-10.10.1996	Passage to Portree (via Fort Augustus 8.10.96 and Corpach, Caledonian Canal 9.10.96)
10.10.1996-22.12.1996	Portree (rlvg ON.1214)
22.12.1996-4.1.1997	Portree (ER)
4.1.1997-6.1.1997	Passage to Buckie (via Lochinver 4.1.97 and Stromness 5.1.97)
6.1.1997	Buckie Bt Yd , Buckie (std; passage crew were from Broughty Ferry who were able to do an RYA Yacht Masters Course whilst passage)

Notable rescue

On 3 September 1983, *Thomas James King* was launched at 3.39am from St Helier to go to a yacht reported firing red flares. The wind was blowing force 8, gusting to gale force 9 at the harbour entrance. Once out of the harbour, Coxswain Michael Berry set a course for St Clement's Bay, where the casualty, the yacht *Cythara*, had been sighted.

Speed was reduced by the lifeboat as she approached Round Rouget Islet, and a searchlight was manned to assist in locating the casualty. The lifeboat crew found the yacht pitching heavily, with three people on deck, surrounded by rocks over which confused seas were breaking. Coxswain Berry had taken the lifeboat three miles between rocks, on a falling tide, in high following seas.

The lifeboat was taken alongside the yacht, and the lifeboatmen grabbed the three crew and took them into the lifeboat's aft cabin. As Coxswain Berry started to manoeuvre clear of the yacht, the lifeboat struck a rock amidships but skilful use of the engines carried her clear.

During the difficult return passage to station, the lifeboat again struck the bottom as she was slowly taken out of the rocks. As she was stuck fast, both ahead and astern movements of the engines were needed to bring her clear. Once free, Coxswain Berry was concerned about inflicting further damage on the lifeboat and in relatively deep water dropped anchor. This enabled the Coxswain to assess the lifeboat's position, as well as check on the survivors.

A route to seaward was found through the rocks, and at 4.40am the anchor was cast off and the lifeboat was steered slowly into deeper water. Acting Mechanic Patrick Attenborough checked the principal compartments of the boat and reported all was well. Course was set for the harbour and at 5.10am the lifeboat reached St Peter Port and headed straight for her mooring. The lifeboat was placed off service pending an inspection of her hull for damage.

For this service carried out in difficult conditions, in which the steel hull of the 44ft Waveney excelled itself, the Silver medal was awarded to Coxswain Berry. The Thanks on Vellum was accorded to Acting Second Coxswain David Aubert, Emergency Mechanic Attenborough, and crew members David Mills, William Hibbs and John Gray.

Disposal

Thomas James King was placed on the sale list on 6 January 1997 and sold out of service in August 1998 to the Montrose Harbour Authority for use as a pilot boat at Montrose docks. Renamed *North Esk,* she remained largely unaltered externally, with a white superstructure and the cabin enclosed, and based in Montrose Docks.

After service, *Thomas James King* became the pilot boat *North Esk* based at Montrose. She was operated as one of several pilot boats and was used to escort ships in and out of the port. She is seen here returning to Montrose in July 2000 after escorting the standby vessel *Viking Seeker* over the bar. (Nicholas Leach)

Key information

Official Number	1035
Year built	1974
Builder	Groves & Guttridge Ltd, Cowes
Yard No.	G&G 665
Cost	£100,000
Weight	18t10

Donor

Proceeds of Irish Lifeboat Appeal.
Named on 14 September 1975 at Dunmore East by Mrs
Peter Barry, wife of the Minister for Transport & Power.

Stations

	Years on station	Record
Dunmore East	19 Mar 1975 – Oct 1996	252/83

Movements

1.1.1974-19.3.1975	Groves & Guttridge, Cowes (building, allocated Dunmore East)
19.3.1975-29.7.1976	Dunmore East (sl)
29.7.1976-20.12.1976	Ocean Fleet's, Birkenhead (rlvd by ON.1005)
20.12.1976-26.9.1980	Dunmore East (sl)
26.9.1980-16.1.1981	Crosshaven Bt Yd, Crosshaven (rlvd by ON.1004)
16.1.1981-21.7.1982	Dunmore East (sl)
21.7.1982-29.10.1982	Tyrells Bt Yd, Arklow (rlvd by ON.849)
29.10.1982-3.6.1984	Dunmore East (sl)
3.6.1984-15.1.1985	Holyhead Bt Yd, Holyhead (rlvd by ON.1004)
15.1.1985-14.5.1986	Dunmore East (sl)
14.5.1986-19.10.1986	Tyrells Bt Yd, Arklow (rlvd by ON.1005)
19.10.1986-10.5.1988	Dunmore East (sl)
10.5.1988-6.9.1988	Tyrells Bt Yd, Arklow (rlvd by ON.1005)
1.1.1989-25.7.1989	Dunmore East (sl)
25.7.1989-14.1.1990	Crosshaven Bt Yd, Crosshaven (S, rlvd by ON.1029 and ON.1005)
14.1.1990-17.12.1990	Dunmore East (sl)
17.12.1990-13.4.1991	Crosshaven Bt Yd, Crosshaven (S, rlvd by ON.1005)
13.4.1991-2.5.1992	Dunmore East (sl)
2.5.1992-22.8.1992	Crosshaven Bt Yd, Crosshaven (S, rlvd by ON.1005)
22.8.1992-20.8.1993	Dunmore East (sl)
20.8.1993-20.11.1993	Crosshaven Bt Yd, Crosshaven (S, rlvd by ON.1003)
20.11.1993-8.10.1994	Dunmore East (sl)
8.10.1994-18.12.1994	Crosshaven Bt Yd, Crosshaven (S, rlvd by ON.1003)
18.12.1994-8.4.1996	Dunmore East (sl)
8.4.1996-23.4.1996	Passage (via Wicklow 8.4.96 and Port Dinorwic 9.4.96)
23.4.1996-7.8.1996	Dickies Bt Yd, Bangor (S)
7.8.1996-14.8.1996	Passage to RNLI Depot, Poole (via Arklow 7.8.96, Dunmore East 8.8.96, Kilmore Quay 9.8.96, Newlyn 10.8.96, Plymouth 12.8.96, Brixham 13.8.96)
14.8.1996-27.4.1999	RNLI Depot, Poole (std, sale list)
27.4.1999-1.6.1999	Souter Marine Ltd, Cowes (hull painted in Australian CG colours)
1.6.1999-3.6.1999	Passage to Tilbury for shipping to Australia (via Eastbourne 1.6.99 and Sheerness 2.6.99)
3.6.1999	Tilbury Dock (for shipping to Australia)

Moored in the middle of the picturesque harbour at Dunmore East in August 1995, *St Patrick* served on Ireland's south-east coast for more then 20 years. (Nicholas Leach)

Notable rescue

Among many notable services carried out by *St Patrick* during her service at Dunmore East, the most arduous took place on 9 July 1976. She was launched at 3.05am under the command of Coxswain Stephen Whittle to an open boat that had gone onto rocks in the early hours of the morning. There was a force 5 wind with frequent heavy rain squalls and it was very dark. Two extra crew were taken as look-outs and to help haul people out of the water if necessary. The area in which the small boat had been reported, Falskirt Rock, was at the foot of 100ft high cliffs with no possible landing place beneath.

To approach the rock, the lifeboat negotiated a very shallow channel known as the Sound during which the crew illuminated the scene with parachute flares and the searchlight. However, the entrance to the channel was blocked by salmon nets and there were hundreds of lobster pots in the area. Coxswain Whittle therefore took *St Patrick* south and approached the area from the south-west.

As the lifeboat approached the cliffs, it was communicated to the lifeboat men that the casualty was close by. Coxswain Whittle slowly took the lifeboat into the Inner Channel where he could see the casualty fast on the rocks. A line was thrown which was reached by one of the survivors who swam to it. He was pulled onto the lifeboat which by this time was operating in less than 20 feet of water and was only 20 feet from the cliffs on which a heavy swell was breaking. Once the survivor had been picked up, the lifeboat had to go astern very fast to avoid the rocks. *St Patrick's* crew then lost sight of the wrecked boat which had been washed clear when the lifeboat went astern. Although Coxswain Whittle took the lifeboat back in to look for the other survivor, there was no sign of either the boat or the other man. The search continued until 11.40am but nothing further was found.

For this service, the Bronze medal was awarded to Coxswain/Mechanic Whittle. Medal service certificates were presented to the remainder of the crew, Second Coxswain John Walsh, Mechanic Joseph Murphy, Assistant Mechanic Brendan Glody and crew members Stanley Power, jnr, Kieran O'Dwyer and Louis O'Dwyer.

Disposal

St Patrick was placed on the sale list on 14 August 1997 and sold out of service on 21 May 1999 to the Royal Volunteer Coastal Patrol, Australia. Renamed *P&O Nedlloyd Strathnaver*, she entered service in the Batemans Bay Division as a Coast Guard vessel and Lifeboat.

Top **At Dunmore East, *St Patrick* at speed.** (T. Power)

Middle **On exercise with an Irish air-sea rescue helicopter, the crew of *St Patrick* watch as the winchman reaches the helicopter safely.** (T. Power)

Bottom **Dressed overall, *St Patrick* at sea off the small Waterford town of Dunmore East.** (T. Power)

Key information

Official Number	1036
Year built	1975
Builder	Groves & Guttridge Ltd, Cowes
Yard No.	G&G 666
Cost	£85,967
Weight	18t4

Donor

Provided by an anonymous gift.
Named on 20 July 1976 at Fleetwood by HRH The Duke of Kent.

Stations

	Years on station	Record
Fleetwood	21 Jan 1976 – 15 Oct 1989	170/95
Dun Laoghaire	20 Mar 1990 – 10 Jan 1995	80/4
Relief	10 Jan 1995 – 2 Nov 1996	4/0

Movements

21.1.1976-13.3.1977	Fleetwood (sl)
13.3.1977-22.7.1977	Bangor Sh Yd, Northern Ireland (S, rlvd by ON.1005)
22.7.1977-12.5.1979	Fleetwood (sl)
12.5.1979-17.6.1979	Bangor Sh Yd, Northern Ireland (S, rlvd by ON.866)
17.6.1979-30.11.1980	Fleetwood (sl)
30.11.1980-9.10.1981	Bangor Sh Yd, Northern Ireland (rlvd by ON.886)
9.10.1981-28.4.1983	Fleetwood (sl)
28.4.1983-30.7.1983	Anglesey Bt Yd, Beaumaris (rlvd by ON.1002)
30.7.1983-5.10.1985	Fleetwood (sl)
5.10.1985-4.2.1986	Anglesey Bt Yd, Beaumaris (rlvd by ON.1004)
4.2.1986-27.7.1987	Fleetwood (sl)
27.7.1987-21.12.1987	Tyrells Bt Yd, Arklow (rlvd by ON.1005)
21.12.1987-12.9.1988	Fleetwood (sl)
12.9.1988-13.9.1988	Passage to Bangor
13.9.1988-4.11.1988	Dickies Bt Yd, Bangor (rlvd by ON.1029)
4.11.1988-15.10.1989	Fleetwood (sl)
15.10.1989-8.1.1990	Fleetwood (replaced by ON.1156, ER)
8.1.1990-19.3.1990	Bangor Sh Yd, Northern Ireland (S)
19.3.1990-20.3.1990	Passage to Dun Laoghaire
20.3.1990-18.4.1991	Dun Laoghaire (TSD)
18.4.1991-1.7.1991	Tyrells Bt Yd, Arklow (rlvd by ON.1005)
1.7.1991-25.8.1992	Dun Laoghaire (TSD)
25.8.1992-4.11.1992	Tyrells Bt Yd, Arklow (S, rlvd by ON.1005)
4.11.1992-14.7.1993	Dun Laoghaire (TSD)
14.7.1993-14.7.1993	Tyrells Bt Yd, Arklow (HC)
14.7.1993-23.11.1993	Dun Laoghaire (TSD)

Dressed overall, *Lady of Lancashire* at sea off Fleetwood on 20 July 1976 at the end of her Naming Ceremony, with HRH The Duke of Kent on board. (Jeff Morris)

23.11.1993-30.1.1994	Tyrells Bt Yd, Arklow (S, rlvd by ON.1003)
30.1.1994-10.1.1995	Dun Laoghaire (TSD)
10.1.1995-15.3.1995	Tyrells Bt Yd, Arklow (S, rlvd by ON.1003)
15.3.1995-4.7.1995	Dun Laoghaire (TSD)
4.7.1995-22.1.1996	Dickies Bt Yd, Bangor (std, ER)
22.1.1996-29.1.1996	Conwy Marina (std)
29.1.1996-4.5.1996	Conwy Marina (ER)
4.5.1996-8.5.1996	Passage to Poole (via Fishguard 4.5.96, Padstow 5.5.96, Salcombe 6.5.96, Brixham 7.5.96)
8.5.1996-2.11.1996	RNLI Depot, Poole (std)
2.11.1996	Left Poole (after sale to Berwick Harbour Commissioners)

Notable rescue

Lady of Lancashire gave excellent service at Fleetwood and performed 170 services, the majority of which were essentially of a routine nature. On 6 March 1989 she was involved, with six other lifeboats, as well as helicopters, aircraft, fishing vessels, merchant vessels and HMS *Ribble*, in an extensive search for the Belgian trawler *Tijl Uilenspiegal*. The trawler was lost with all hands and a large search was mounted. *Lady of Lancashire* launched at 11.08am to join the search, and returned to station at 8.04pm having found nothing. For their help in this extensive search, Letters of Appreciation signed by the RNLI Chief of Operations, Commodore George Cooper, were sent to the lifeboat stations involved, including Fleetwood.

Disposal

Lady of Lancashire was placed on the sale list on 8 May 1996 and out of service in November 1996 for £55,000 to Berwick Harbour Commissioners for use as a Pilot Boat at Berwick. She was the first Waveney to be sold out of service, and became the third ex-lifeboat owned by the Commissioners. Renamed *St Boisel,* the wheelhouse was enclosed aft, apart from which she remained largely unaltered and was operated as the Berwick pilot boat.

Top   On trials, *Lady of Lancashire* at speed shortly after being built. (RNLI)

Middle   *Lady of Lancashire* on exercise off Fleetwood. (From a postcard in the author's collection)

Bottom   Renamed *St Boisel* and in use as a pilot boat, *Lady of Lancashire* moored at Berwick-upon-Tweed in October 1997. The aft end of her wheelhouse was fully enclosed for her new duties. (Nicholas Leach)

Key information

Official Number	1042
Year built	1976
Builder	Bideford Shipyard, North Devon
Yard No.	Y 59
Cost	£130,000
Weight	19t

Donor

Legacy of Mrs A G Cranthorne and RNLI Funds; named after Cdr F R H Swann, CBE, RNVR, of Salisbury, Wilts, Chairman and a Life Vice President of the RNLI; and donor of echo sounder, Mrs G O McClaren, Ashford, Kent.

Named on 23 September 1976 at Ramsgate by HRH Duchess of Kent, after a former Chairman of the RNLI, Commander Ralph Swann and his late wife.

Stations

	Years on station	Record
Ramsgate	14 July 1976 – Apr 1990	292/199
Tobermory	6 Aug 1990 – Feb 1991	14/2
Portree	2 May 1991 – June 1996	60/4
Relief	June 1996 – 1998	13/1

Movements

7.1976	Passage to Ramsgate (1/0)
14.7.1976-4.4.1978	Ramsgate (sl)
4.4.1978-24.6.1978	Brown's Bt Yd, Rowhedge (S, rlvd by 44-001)
24.6.1978-30.7.1979	Ramsgate (sl)
24.9.1979-25.2.1980	Brown's Bt Yd, Rowhedge (S, rlvd by ON.849)
25.2.1980-27.5.1981	Ramsgate (sl)
27.5.1981-28.5.1981	Passage to Cowes
28.5.1981-18.1.1982	FBM Marine Ltd, Cowes (S, RE, rlvd by ON.1043)
18.1.1982-22.1.1982	Extended passage to Ramsgate
22.1.1982-26.6.1983	Ramsgate (sl)
26.6.1983-3.7.1983	FBM Marine Ltd, Cowes (M, rlvd by ON.948)
3.7.1983-30.9.1983	Ramsgate (sl)
30.9.1983-3.3.1984	Fletchers Bt Yd, Lowestoft (S)
3.3.1984-21.1.1986	Ramsgate (sl)
21.1.1986-2.5.1986	Crescent Marine, Otterham Quay (S, rlvd by ON.1045)
2.5.1986-25.2.1988	Ramsgate (sl)
25.2.1988-8.7.1988	Crescent Marine, Otterham Quay (S, rlvd by ON.1003)
8.7.1988-2.11.1989	Ramsgate (sl)
2.11.1989-14.2.1990	Crescent Marine, Otterham Quay (S, rlvd by ON.1002)
14.2.1990-16.2.1990	Great Yarmouth & Gorleston (rlvg ON.1065)
16.2.1990-3.5.1990	Crescent Marine, Otterham Quay (std)
3.5.1990-5.5.1990	Passage to RNLI Depot, Poole
5.5.1990-18.5.1990	RNLI Depot, Poole (Tobermory CT)
18.5.1990-24.5.1990	Passage to Tobermory
24.5.1990-25.6.1990	Tobermory (T; TSD for station evaluation)
25.6.1990-10.7.1990	Oban (R; Tobermory CT temporarily suspended)
10.7.1990-6.8.1990	Tobermory (CT)
6.8.1990-14.2.1991	Tobermory (TSD)
14.2.1991-15.2.1991	Passage to Buckie, calling at Caledonian Canal
15.2.1991-27.4.1991	Herd & Mackenzie, Buckie (S)
27.4.1991-29.4.1991	Passage to Portree (via Stromness 27.4.91, Lochinver 28.4.91)
29.4.1991-2.5.1991	Portree (CT)
2.5.1991-18.8.1991	Portree (TSD)
31.7.1991-3.8.1991	Kyle Naval Slipway (R, rlvd by ON.1034)
18.8.1991-30.8.1991	Kyle of Lochalsh (awaiting passage to Buckie)
30.8.1991-1.9.1991	Passage to Buckie
1.9.1991-12.10.1991	Herd & Mackenzie, Buckie (S, rlvd by ON.1034)
12.10.1991-13.10.1991	Passage to Portree
13.10.1991-20.1.1993	Portree (TSD)
20.1.1993-22.1.1993	Passage to Buckie

Dressed overall, *Ralph and Joy Swann* **seen entering Ramsgate harbour at the end of her Naming Ceremony on 23 September 1976. (Jeff Morris)**

While stationed at Ramsgate, *Ralph and Joy Swann* **performed many fine rescues on the notorious Goodwin Sands. (From a postcard in the author's collection)**

22.1.1993-22.3.1993	Herd & Mackenzie, Buckie (S, rlvd by ON.1034)
22.3.1993-24.3.1993	Passage to Portree
24.3.1993-4.11.1993	Portree (TSD)
4.11.1993-4.11.1993	Passage to Kyle of Lochalsh
4.11.1993-4.11.1993	Kyle of Lochalsh Naval Slip (HC)
4.11.1993-4.11.1993	Passage to Portree
4.11.1993-12.3.1994	Portree (TSD)
12.3.1994-18.3.1994	Passage to Rosneath, via Oban
18.3.1994-20.5.1994	Silver Marine, Rosneath (S, rlvd by ON.1006)
20.5.1994-21.5.1994	Passage (via Crinan Canal)
21.5.1994-22.5.1994	Passage (via Tobermory)
22.5.1994-5.3.1995	Portree (TSD)
5.3.1995-7.3.1995	Passage (via Corpach, Caledonian Canal 5.3.95 and Fort Augustus 6.3.95)
7.3.1995-8.5.1995	Jones Bt Yd, Buckie (S, rlvd by ON.1006)
8.5.1995-10.5.1995	Passage (via Caledonian Canal)
10.5.1995-21.11.1995	Portree (TSD)
21.11.1995-21.11.1995	BUTEC, Kyle of Lochalsh (HC)
21.11.1995-7.6.1996	Portree (TSD)
7.6.1996-9.6.1996	Passage to Rosneath (via Oban 7.6.96 and Loch Tarbert 8.6.96)
9.6.1996-8.9.1996	Silver Marine, Rosneath (S)
8.9.1996-9.9.1996	Passage to Dun Laoghaire (via Donaghadee)
9.9.1996-21.10.1996	Dun Laoghaire (rlvg ON.1200)
21.10.1996-22.10.1996	Passage to Rosneath (via Portpatrick)
22.10.1996-26.1.1997	Silver Marine, Rosneath (std)
26.1.1997-27.1.1997	Passage to Achill (via Campbeltown)
27.1.1997-28.1.1997	Passage to Achill (via Arranmore)
28.1.1997-2.2.1997	Achill Island (rlvg ON.1027)
2.2.1997-4.2.1997	Passage to Bangor Marina (via Arranmore 2.2.97 and Portrush 3.2.97)
4.2.1997-28.2.1997	Bangor Marina (R)
28.2.1997-2.3.1997	Passage to Portree (via Islay 28.2.97 and Tobermory 1.3.97)
2.3.1997-28.3.1997	Portree (rlvg ON.1214)
28.3.1997-5.4.1997	Portree (awaiting passage to Larne)
5.4.1997-6.4.1997	Passage to Larne (via Oban)
6.4.1997-22.6.1997	Larne (rlvg ON.1079)
22.7.1997-24.7.1997	Passage to Achill (via Portrush 22.7.97 and Ballyglass 23.7.97)
24.7.1997-15.2.1998	Achill Island (rlvg ON.1027)
15.2.1998-18.2.1998	Fenit (awaiting passage crew)
18.2.1998-24.2.1998	Passage to Poole (via Baltimore 19.2.98, Dunmore East 20.2.98, delayed due to weather conditions 21.2.98, Padstow 22.2.98, Newlyn 23.2.98, Salcombe 24.2.98)
24.2.1998-1.4.1998	RNLI Depot, Poole (on sale list)
1.4.1998-4.4.1998	RNLI Depot, Poole (T)
4.4.1998-28.8.1998	RNLI Depot, Poole (PR trip for Portuguese Rescue Society)
28.8.1998	Loaded in Marchwood, Southampton (for shipment to West Falkland Islands)

Notable rescue

Ralph and Joy Swann was involved in an outstanding service on 26 December 1985 which began after a message was received at Ramsgate that the French trawler *Gloire à Marie II* was aground south of the port and in need of urgent assistance. The wind, already gale force 9, increased to a north easterly violent storm force 11. To board the lifeboat, which was moored in the outer harbour, Coxswain/Mechanic Ron Cannon used his father's 35ft workboat, with the first three crew members to arrive, rather than use the station's own boarding board.

Once on board, *Ralph and Joy Swann* was brought alongside the East Pier steps and other crew members were picked up. With seas reaching more than 30 feet in height at the harbour entrance, Coxswain/Mechanic Cannon checked all the crew individually to make sure lifejackets and protective clothing were being properly worn. *Ralph and Joy Swann* made her way to the harbour entrance at 8.15pm and was driven out into violent short cross seas. Once clear of the harbour, a course was set for the trawler with the lifeboat pitching and rolling heavily.

At 10.25pm the casualty was seen aground in shoal water off the entrance to the river Stour. The irregular seas made the lifeboat difficult to control and a constant watch astern was maintained to warn the Coxswain if a steep sea approached. In order to help the casualty, two lifeboatmen were put on board. Getting the lifeboat alongside the trawler required considerable skill and the heavy seas meant that several attempts had to be abandoned.

The skipper of the trawler did not want to abandon his vessel, particularly as it was seaworthy and the main engines were available. So Coxswain/Mechanic Cannon attempted to tow her off the sandbank on which she was stuck. A 60 fathom towline was passed aboard the trawler, and then the Coxswain slowly began pulling the trawler's head round to the south, while keeping the lifeboat head to sea. This extremely difficult manoeuvre was skilfully executed using the lifeboat's capabilities. Twice, the heavy seas caused the towline to part, but it was reconnected.

Once the trawler was clear of the sandbank, her engines were started and under her own power was led to Ramsgate by *Ralph and Joy Swann*. Both vessels entered the harbour at 9.30pm and moored in the lee of the east pier. Those in the harbour could not remember worse weather than on this night. Nine boats sank at their moorings inside the harbour, and buildings on the east pier suffered structural damage.

For this outstanding service, the Silver medal was awarded to Coxswain/Mechanic Cannon. Silver medal service certificates were presented to the remainder of the crew, Second Coxswain Derek Pagden, and crew members Ronald Blay, Alan Bray, Michael Petts, Nigel Stephens, Ray Noble and John Cheeseman.

Disposal

Ralph and Joy Swann was placed on the sale list on 24 February 1998 and sold out of service in July 1998 to Robin Lee, of Port Howard Lodge, Falkland Islands. She was shipped from Poole to the Falklands in Autumn 1998, and arrived at Port Stanley in October 1998. She was then sailed across to Port Howard, on West Falkland, a 10 hour journey, where her new owner operated a Tourist Lodge and 200,000 acre sheep farm. She was renamed *West Swann* after an island in the Falkland Sound. The double 'n' in Swann was retained to maintain a link with her old name. During the season, she was used to take tourists on trips to see the penguins, dolphins and other wildlife and seabirds on the smaller islands, as well as some inshore fishing. She was also used as a ferry to take people and freight across Falkland Sound to Port San Carlos on East Falkland to pick up supplies and guests for the Lodge. In December 1999, Mr Lee was married at a remote shepherd shanty on the North coast of West Falkland. The couple were going to use *West Swann* to take them on their honeymoon, but in the end a smaller boat was more practical. In January 2000 Mr Lee started suffering heart problems, and he was flown to the United Kingdom in March for treatment. Sadly, on 9 May he died of a massive heart attack, having been married for less than five months. *West Swann* remains at Port Howard, and is now operated by Myles Lee, Mr Lee's eldest son.

Top left   In the Outer Harbour at Ramsgate in July 1982, *Ralph and Joy Swann* at her usual moorings. (Tony Denton)

Middle   In 1990 a new lifeboat station was established at Tobermory, and the first lifeboat to be stationed there was *Ralph and Joy Swann*. She is seen here arriving on station in May 1990 ready to take up her new duties. Although a lifeboat had first operated at Tobermory in 1938, this was withdrawn in 1947. The station was reopened following a reappraisal of rescue coverage in the Western Isles. (RNLI)

Left   Moored in the picturesque harbour at Portree, Skye, in 1995, *Ralph and Joy Swann* was the first lifeboat ever to operate from the Isle of Skye. (Nicholas Leach)

Seen here in West Falkland after being sold out of service, *Ralph and Joy Swann* is now based in the Falkland Islands and has been renamed *West Swann* by her new owners. (Hattie Lee)

Key information

Official Number	1043
Year built	1976
Builder	Bideford Shipyard, North Devon
Yard No.	Y60
Cost	£174,688
Weight	18t10

Donor

Various legacies plus local appeal, but never formally named *The Nelsons of Donaghadee*. Reappropriated in 1980 to the gift of the Wavy Line Grocers Association, and reallocated to the Relief Fleet.
Named on 3 September 1980, at St Katherine's Dock, London, by Mrs Barbara Laird, wife of a Wavy Line grocer from Hartley Wintney.

Stations

Stations	Years on station	Record
Donaghadee	Oct 1976 – July 1977	1/0
Relief	1978 – 1990	111/51
Sunderland	17 Apr 1990 – 28 Mar 1997	113/20
Relief	28 Mar 1997 – 6 Mar 1998	0/0

Movements

ON.1043 was allocated to Donaghadee as *The Nelsons of Donaghadee* and was station lifeboat from 1.12.1976. However, she developed mechanical faults and so was reallocated to the relief fleet. ON.885 *Sir Samuel Kelly* remained at Donaghadee temporarily.

10.10.1976-12.10.1976	40 hour trials (allocated to Donaghadee)
12.10.1976-23.10.1976	Passage from RNLI Depot, Poole, to Donaghadee
23.10.1976-17.12.1976	Donaghadee (rlvd ON.885: 1/0)
17.12.1976-31.12.1976	Bangor Sh Yd, Northern Ireland (std)
31.12.1976-17.7.1977	Donaghadee (ER)
17.7.1977-21.7.1977	Passage to RNLI Depot, Poole
21.7.1977-1.10.1977	RNLI Depot, Poole (std, T)
1.10.1977-3.10.1977	Passage to Plymouth
3.10.1977-10.10.1977	Mashford's Bt Yd, Plymouth (S)
10.10.1977-11.10.1977	RNLI Depot, Poole
11.10.1977-22.11.1977	Branksea Marine, Wareham (M)
22.11.1977-25.11.1977	RNLI Depot, Poole (engine trials in Solent)
25.11.1977-7.2.1978	Wm Osborne, Littlehampton (RE, trials service 26.1.78: 1/0)
7.2.1978-10.2.1978	Yarmouth (T, in Solent as guard for Atlantic 21)
10.2.1978-14.2.1978	Wm Osborne, Littlehampton (M)
14.2.1978-4.3.1978	Extended passage to Poole
4.3.1978-18.8.1978	RNLI Depot, Poole (std)
18.8.1978-12.1.1979	Wm Osborne, Littlehampton (M)
12.1.1979-13.1.1979	FBM Marine Ltd, Cowes (SRT)
13.1.1979-22.1.1979	Passage and further trials
22.1.1979-21.8.1979	Wm Osborne, Littlehampton (std)
21.8.1979-27.8.1979	Passage to Poole (T)
27.8.1979-29.8.1979	RNLI Depot, Poole
29.8.1979-4.9.1979	Passage to St Peter Port (T)
4.9.1979-23.9.1979	St Peter Port (rlvg ON.1025: 1/0)
23.9.1979-10.10.1979	RNLI Depot, Poole (ER)
10.10.1979-30.6.1980	FBM Marine Ltd, Cowes (S, RE)
30.6.1980-30.7.1980	FBM Marine Ltd, Cowes (T)
30.7.1980-2.8.1980	RNLI Depot, Poole (T, passage service 30.7.80: 1/6 and yacht)
2.8.1980-5.8.1980	Passage to RNLI Depot, Poole (via Brixham and Weymouth; passage service 3.8.80: 1/2)
5.8.1980-28.8.1980	RNLI Depot, Poole (ER)
28.8.1980-5.9.1980	Passage to London for Naming Ceremony (via Newhaven)
2.9.1980-5.9.1980	St Katherine's Dock, London, for Naming Ceremony on 3.9.1980
5.9.1980-28.11.1980	Newhaven (rlvg ON.1045: 4/0)
28.11.1980-26.4.1981	Dover (rlvg ON.1031: 9/5)
26.4.1981-27.4.1981	Passage to Rowhedge
27.4.1981-22.5.1981	Brown's Bt Yd, Rowhedge (S)
22.5.1981-25.1.1982	Ramsgate (rlvd ON.1042: 24/13)
25.1.1982-28.1.1982	Passage to South Shields
28.1.1982-19.3.1982	Coastal Marine, Eyemouth (S, ER)
19.3.1982-19.2.1983	Hartlepool (rlvg ON.1044: 7/0)
19.2.1983-24.6.1983	Eyemouth (rlvg ON.1026: 2/3)

The Naming Ceremony of *Wavy Line* at St Katherine's Dock, London, on 3 September 1980. (Jeff Morris)

The champagne bottle breaks over the bows of *Wavy Line* at the end of her Naming Ceremony in 1980. (Jeff Morris)

24.6.1983-13.9.1983	Whitby (rlvg ON.1033: 6/10)
13.9.1983-20.9.1983	Blyth (rlvg ON.1079)
20.9.1983-22.9.1983	Passage to Humber
22.9.1983-29.9.1983	Humber (rlvg ON.1052: 3/0)
29.9.1983-30.9.1983	Passage to Ramsgate
30.9.1983-26.3.1984	Ramsgate (rlvg ON.1042: 9/10)
26.3.1984-20.10.1984	Brown's Bt Yd, Rowhedge (ER)
20.10.1984-21.10.1984	Passage to Hartlepool
21.10.1984-8.12.1984	Hartlepool (rlvg ON.1044: 2/0)
8.12.1984-9.3.1985	Eyemouth (rlvg ON.1026: 2/3)
9.3.1985-10.3.1985	Passage to Whitby
10.3.1985-25.7.1985	Whitby (rlvg ON.1033: 6/0)
25.7.1985-15.10.1985	Blyth (rlvg ON.1079)
15.10.1985-24.1.1986	Robson's Bt Yd, South Shields (ER)
24.1.1986-10.5.1986	Hartlepool (rlvg ON.1044: 2/0)
10.5.1986-19.9.1986	Eyemouth (rlvg ON.1026)
19.9.1986-20.9.1986	Passage to Whitby
20.9.1986-19.2.1987	Whitby (rlvg ON.1033: 14/0)
19.2.1987-10.4.1987	Blyth (rlvg ON.1079: 2/0)
10.4.1987-8.6.1987	Amble (rlvg ON.1004: 1/0)
8.6.1987-20.8.1987	Hartlepool (rlvg ON.1044: 3/0)
20.8.1987-24.10.1987	Amble Boat Company Ltd (ER)
24.10.1987-16.1.1988	Eyemouth (rlvg ON.1026: 0/0)
16.1.1988-18.3.1988	Blyth (rlvg ON.1079: 1/1)
18.3.1988-23.7.1988	Amble (rlvg ON.1004: 4/0)
23.7.1988-9.10.1988	Hartlepool (rlvg ON.1044: 5/0)
9.10.1988-17.12.1988	Robson's Bt Yd, South Shields (ER)
17.12.1988-30.4.1989	Eyemouth (rlvg ON.1026: 5/2)
30.4.1989-25.6.1989	Blyth (rlvg ON.1079)
25.6.1989-14.7.1989	Amble (rlvg ON.1004)
14.7.1989-20.10.1989	Amble Marina (ER)
20.10.1989-20.12.1989	Hartlepool (rlvg ON.1044: 1/0)
20.12.1989-27.3.1990	Amble Bt Co, Amble (S, reallocated Sunderland)
27.3.1990-31.3.1990	Passage to Poole
31.3.1990-7.4.1990	RNLI Depot, Poole (Sunderland CT)
7.4.1990-10.4.1990	Passage to Sunderland
10.4.1990-17.4.1990	Sunderland (CT)
17.4.1990-13.4.1991	Sunderland (sl, officially on service from 17.4.90)
13.4.1991-15.6.1991	Amble Bt Co, Amble (S, rlvd by ON.1001)
15.6.1991-27.6.1992	Sunderland (sl)
27.6.1992-12.9.1992	Amble Bt Co, Amble (S, rlvd ON.1001)
12.9.1992-28.2.1993	Sunderland (sl)
28.2.1993-4.3.1993	Teesmouth (temporary cover after Hartlepool lifeboat capsize)
4.3.1993-23.6.1993	Sunderland (back on station, via Amble, escorting Hartlepool LB)
23.6.1993-30.6.1993	Local Bt Yd (R, rlvd by ON.1001)
30.6.1993-18.8.1993	Sunderland (sl)
18.8.1993-13.11.1993	Amble Bt Co, Amble (S, rlvd by ON.1001)
13.11.1993-15.10.1994	Sunderland (sl)
15.10.1994-3.12.1994	Amble Bt Co, Amble (S, rlvd by ON.1001)
3.12.1994-6.12.1994	Sunderland (not on station due to gearbox failure)
6.12.1994-21.1.1995	Amble Bt Co, Amble (R)
21.1.1995-5.10.1995	Sunderland (sl)
5.10.1995-5.10.1995	Robson's Bt Yd, Sth Shields (HC)
5.10.1995-27.3.1996	Sunderland (sl)
27.3.1996-30.7.1996	Amble Boat Company Ltd (S, rlvd by ON1001)
30.7.1996-28.3.1997	Sunderland (awaiting completion of new moorings)
28.3.1997-21.4.1997	Sunderland (sl)
21.4.1997-25.4.1997	Passage to RNLI Depot, Poole (via Scarborough 21.4.97, Gorleston 22.4.97, Ramsgate 23.4.97, Newhaven 24.4.97)
25.4.1997-5.3.1998	RNLI Depot, Poole (std)
5.3.1998-7.3.1998	Passage to Tilbury Docks (via Sheerness, final passage under RNLI flag)

Notable rescues

During service in the Relief Fleet, *Wavy Line* carried out rescues at many different stations. Two of the most notable occurred during 1983. The first took place on 25 March when she was on duty at Eyemouth. At 1.25pm she was launched to the trawler *Hatcliffe*, of Grimsby, under the command of Coxswain Alexander Dougal, in very rough seas, with a NNE gale gusting to force 9. Coxswain Dougal had to reduce speed as the lifeboat cleared St Abbs Head, but the casualty was reached at 1.50pm.

The trawler had broken down and another fishing vessel, *Heather Joy*, was attempting to get a line on board the casualty. Once the lifeboat was on the scene, Coxswain Dougal skilfully manoeuvred her towards the disabled boat and got a tow line on board at the first attempt. The lifeboat then made for St Abbs, but conditions there were so bad that they were unable to enter the harbour. Coxswain Dougal then made for Berwick-upon-Tweed, but there too conditions were impossible and a member of the local lifeboat crew advised against trying to cross the harbour entrance where an extremely heavy swell had built up.

The weather was deteriorating and storm force 10 winds were forecast. With Eyemouth harbour closed to all shipping, Coxswain Dougal decided to make for Burnmouth. Changing directions with two boats was a difficult procedure, but slowly the lifeboat was brought round and pulled the casualty with her. Despite the heavy pounding both boats received in the severe conditions, they reached Burnmouth at 8.35pm. Minutes later, however, the tow line parted, and it took a with considerable effort on the part of the lifeboat men to reconnect it.

At 9.15pm both boats entered Burnmouth harbour after the tow line had been shortened to enable the fishing vessel to be safely manoeuvred near the harbour entrance. Once safely in the harbour, both boats were moored up. The lifeboat was left there overnight and her crew returned home by road. For this service a Framed Letter of Appreciation signed by the RNLI Chairman, His Grace The Duke of Atholl, was presented to Coxswain Dougal and the crew, Second Coxswain/Mechanic James Tarvit, Assistant Mechanic James Dougal and crew members Andrew Redden, John Buchan, John Purves and Ian Dougal.

The second notable rescue of 1983 took place on 29 October when *Wavy Line* was on duty at Ramsgate. She

launched at 11.14pm under the command of Coxswain Ron Cannon after red flares had been sighted to the south-east of Ramsgate. In a force 5 wind, the lifeboatmen searched the area using the parachute flares, spotting the casualty, the 26ft yacht *Mer Gespard*, of Belgium, around midnight. With six people on board, she was hard aground, and heavy seas were repeatedly breaking over her deck.

Wavy Line was slowly taken towards the casualty, striking the bottom several times as seas swept over her. Coxswain Cannon then skilfully manoeuvred the lifeboat up to the yacht and held her bow against the yacht's quarter enabling all six people on the yacht to be got to safety. Second Coxswain Derek Pegden was then put on board the yacht taking a tow line with him. When the lifeboat was in deeper water, the line was made fast and the yacht was pulled clear. At 12.35am the return passage to Ramsgate began where both boats arrived safely at 1.15am.

For this rescue, a Framed Letter of Appreciation signed by the RNLI Chairman, His Grace The Duke of Atholl, was sent to Coxswain Cannon and the crew Second Coxswain Pegden, Emergency Mechanic Dennis Cooper and crew members William Blay, Thomas Brown and Tim Hurst.

Disposal

Wavy Line was placed on the sale list on 25 April 1997 and sold out of service on 7 March 1998 to the Royal New Zealand Coastguard Federation for search and rescue based at Mana Island, near Wellington. She was shipped out from Tilbury free of charge by P&O Nedlloyd on the *Pegasus Bay*, the first of six Waveneys to go to New Zealand. During passage to Gravesend for shipment, problems were encountered on the last leg of the journey. The fuel filters were blocked, followed by a broken return fuel pipe on the port engine-this in turn created a problem at the loading berth holding the boat on station whilst the lift was carried out. The actual lift was delayed until slack water but the boat was finally lifted with the aid of a work boat.

She arrived in Wellington at 11am on Sunday 30 April 1998, was unloaded at the container terminal free of charge by the Port of Wellington, and is now based at Mana Marina in Porirua harbour, Paremata, about 20 kilometres by road from Wellington. The boat was funded by a grant from the Lottery's Grants Board and by Porirua Licensing Trust. The Trust gave the naming rights to their trading arm, Nicholsons and so the boat was named *Nicholsons Rescue*. However, Nicholsons went into receivership in August 1999 and a new sponsorship deal with the Trust was finalised in April 2000 so the boat was renamed *Trust Porirua Rescue*.

Top   On relief duty at Blyth in September 1983, *Wavy Line* stands in during the Naming Ceremony of Blyth's own Waveney, *The William and Jane*. (Jeff Morris)

Upper middle   When *Wavy Line* was first stationed at Sunderland, she was kept at these moorings on the South Side of the river, close to the lifeboat house. (Nicholas Leach)

Lower middle and bottom   In 1995, moorings were moved to the North Side of the river, and *Wavy Line* was kept here until being replaced in 1997. (Nicholas Leach)

Key information

Official Number	1044
Year built	1977
Builder	Bideford Shipyard
Yard No.	Y 61
Cost	£122,000
Weight	18t18

Donor

The Scout Association.
Named on 14 July 1977 at Hartlepool by HM Queen Elizabeth II.

Stations

Stations	Years on station	Record
Hartlepool	17 Feb 1977 – July 1997	250/10

Movements

1.1.1976-9.12.1976	Bideford Shipyard (under construction)
9.12.1976-11.12.1976	Passage to Poole (via Newlyn and Falmouth)
11.12.1976-30.3.1977	RNLI Depot, Poole (trials, including fuel, speed and noise trials from Poole to Stokes Bay)
30.3.1977-30.3.1977	Passage from Poole to Cowes
30.3.1977-5.4.1977	FBM Marine Ltd, Cowes (M)
5.4.1977-14.4.1977	RNLI Depot, Poole (T)
14.4.1977-25.4.1977	Passage to Hartlepool and back
25.4.1977-13.5.1977	RNLI Depot, Poole (ER, T)
13.5.1977-18.6.1977	Wm Osborne, Littlehampton (S, I)
18.6.1977-21.6.1977	Passage to Hartlepool (CT)
21.6.1977-14.7.1977	Hartlepool (at station)
14.7.1977-12.9.1978	Hartlepool (sl)
12.9.1978-28.10.1978	Harrisons, Amble (S, rlvd by ON.910)
28.10.1978-15.10.1979	Hartlepool (sl)
15.10.1979-29.2.1980	Harrisons, Amble (S, rlvd by ON.962)
29.2.1980-18.6.1981	Hartlepool (sl)
18.6.1981-16.7.1981	Robson's Bt Yd, South Shields (S, rlvd by ON.962)
16.7.1981-5.4.1982	Hartlepool (sl)
5.4.1982-9.4.1982	Passage to Cowes
9.4.1982-10.1.1983	FBM Marine Ltd, Cowes (RE, M, rlvd by ON.1043)
10.1.1983-21.1.1983	RNLI Depot, Poole (T)
21.1.1983-25.1.1983	Passage (40hr trials)
25.1.1983-2.2.1983	FBM Marine Ltd, Cowes (T, M)
2.2.1983-5.2.1983	Passage to Hartlepool
5.2.1983-8.2.1983	Hartlepool (T)
8.2.1983-14.2.1983	Robson's Bt Yd, South Shields (M and I, rlvd by ON.1043)
14.2.1983-29.10.1984	Hartlepool (sl)
29.10.1984-3.12.1984	Robson's Bt Yd, South Shields (S, rlvd by ON.1043)
3.12.1984-19.11.1985	Hartlepool (sl)
19.11.1985-28.11.1985	Robson's Bt Yd, South Shields (S, rlvd by 44-001)
28.11.1985-28.1.1986	Hartlepool (sl)
28.1.1986-6.5.1986	Robson's Bt Yd, South Shields (S, rlvd by ON.1043)
6.5.1986-9.6.1987	Hartlepool (sl)
9.6.1987-19.8.1987	Amble Bt Co, Amble (S, rlvd by ON.1043)
19.8.1987-24.7.1988	Hartlepool (sl)
24.7.1988-8.10.1988	Amble Bt Co, Amble (S, rlvd by ON.1043)
8.10.1988-22.10.1989	Hartlepool (sl)
22.10.1989-19.12.1989	Amble Bt Co, Amble (S, rlvd by ON.1043)
19.12.1989-19.12.1990	Hartlepool (sl)
19.12.1990-10.4.1991	Amble Bt Co, Amble (S, rlvd by ON.1001)
10.4.1991-5.4.1992	Hartlepool (sl)
5.4.1992-20.6.1992	Amble Bt Co, Amble (S, rlvd by ON.1001)
20.6.1992-28.2.1993	Hartlepool (sl)
28.2.1993-28.2.1993	Hartlepool (capsized on service, off service while damage assessed)
28.2.1993-4.3.1993	Redcar Marina, Teesmouth (off service, rlvd by 44-001)

Dressed overall, *The Scout* before her Naming Ceremony at Hartlepool in July 1977. (Supplied by R W Williams)

Hartlepool crew and station officials on board *The Scout*, with Atlantic 21 *Burton Brewer* (B-568). (R W Williams)

4.3.1993-1.8.1993	Amble Bt Co, Amble (R, rlvd by 44-001)
1.8.1993-13.8.1994	Hartlepool (sl)
13.8.1994-8.10.1994	Amble Bt Co, Amble (S)
8.10.1994-14.1.1996	Hartlepool (sl)
14.1.1996-24.3.1996	Amble Bt Co, Amble (S, rlvd by ON.1001)
24.3.1996-1.7.1997	Hartlepool (sl)
1.7.1997-3.7.1997	Local Bt Yd (R, ON.1131 TSD)
3.7.1997-29.9.1997	Hartlepool (ON.1131 used for CT)
29.9.1997-4.10.1997	Passage to RNLI Depot, Poole (via Scarborough 30.9.97, Gorleston 1.10.97, Ramsgate 2.10.97, Yarmouth 3.10.97)
4.10.1997-20.10.1997	RNLI Depot, Poole (std)
20.10.1997-14.11.1997	RNLI Depot, Poole (T)
14.11.1997-18.11.1997	Passage to Tilbury Docks (via Newhaven 15.11.97, Ramsgate 16.11.97, Sheerness 17.11.97)
18.11.1997	Sold to Uruguayan Lifeboat Service

Notable rescue

Late on the night of 9 November 1985, the Dutch motor vessel *Anne* radioed that she was dragging her anchor and getting close to Long Scar rocks near Hartlepool. The wind, strong gale force 9, was gusting to force 11. By 12.10am on 10 November the vessel was aground on the rocks, and five minutes later *The Scout* left her berth at Hartlepool with Coxswain Robbie Maiden at the helm.

Once clear of the breakwater, the full force of the very high breaking seas forced the coxswain to reduce speed. At 12.30am the lifeboat reached the casualty, which was hard aground with heavy seas breaking across her decks. The casualty was waiting for a tug, and so Coxswain Maiden decided to stand by in deep water to the south of the rocks.

When tugs were forced to turn back because of the weather, a Sea King helicopter was scrambled from RAF Boulmer. The helicopter stood by, and at 1.50am five men emerged from the coaster's accommodation at the stern and waved the lifeboat in. In the lee of the rocks, the waves moderated to 10 to 15 feet. When first positioned alongside, a heavy sea pushed the lifeboat away. A second attempt to get alongside was more successful, and two men were taken off before another large sea swept the lifeboat's bow off and pushed her starboard quarter on to the coaster's stern. The collision damaged the lifeboat's after cabin housing.

The damage was relatively superficial and so the coxswain made another run to the same position enabling two more crew members to be taken off. The lifeboat then stood off astern with the four seamen aboard. After half an hour, with the tide falling, the coaster's captain was out of immediate

danger and the lifeboat headed back to Hartlepool where the men were landed at 3.06am.

For this service, the Bronze medal was awarded to Coxswain Maiden. Medal service certificates were awarded to the remainder of the crew, Second Coxswain/Mechanic David Wilson, Assistant Mechanic Oswald Rennie and crew members Eric Reeve, Edward Porritt and Ian Vincent.

Disposal

The Scout was placed on the sale list on 24 July 1997 and sold out of service later in 1997 to ADES, the Uruguay lifeboat service, for service at Base No1 Puerto del Buceo, a suburb of the capital, Montevideo. Transported on a merchant ship from Tilbury Docks to South America, she was renamed *ADES 16 14-016* for service in Uruguay.

Top **At her usual moorings, *The Scout* in the Dock at Hartlepool. (Steve Dutton)**

Middle **Off the South Gare at Teesmouth in July 1996, *The Scout* regularly attended the Teesmouth Lifeboat Day while stationed at nearby Hartlepool. (Nicholas Leach)**

Bottom **Leaving Gorleston in 1997, *The Scout* on passage south to RNLI Depot, Poole, after being replaced at Hartlepool. (Paul Gowen, courtesy of Gary Markham)**

Key information

Official Number	1045
Year built	1977
Builder	Bideford Shipyard
Yard No.	Y 62
Cost	£150,000
Weight	18t14

Donor

Gift of the National Associations of Round Tables, Great Britain and Ireland, in honour of its founder and on the occasion of the Golden Jubilee 1977.
Named on 18 September 1977 at Newhaven by Mrs Bangor-Jones, wife of the National President of Round Tables, Great Britain and Ireland.

Stations

Station	Years on station	Record
Newhaven	24 May 1977 – 9 Aug 1985	289/134
Relief	9 Aug 1985 – Oct 1986	0/0
Alderney	23 Oct 1986 – 7 Mar 1994	170/123
Exmouth	8 July 1994 – 6 July 1996	39/5
Relief	5 Dec 1996 – 20 Apr 1997	1/0

Movements

8.5.1977-24.5.1977	Newhaven (at station)
24.5.1977-24.10.1978	Newhaven (sl)
24.10.1978-23.3.1979	Wm Osborne, Littlehampton (rlvd by ON.821 and ON.910)
23.3.1979-19.12.1979	Newhaven (sl)
19.12.1979-12.1.1980	Crescent Marine, Otterham Quay (rlvd by ON.821)
12.1.1980-8.9.1980	Newhaven (sl)
8.9.1980-27.11.1980	Wm Osborne, Littlehampton (rlvd by ON.1043)
27.11.1980-8.10.1981	Newhaven (sl)
8.10.1981-19.5.1982	Groves & Guttridge, Cowes (RE, rlvd by 44-001)
19.5.1982-23.5.1982	Passage to Newhaven
23.5.1982-18.1.1984	Newhaven (sl)
18.1.1984-27.3.1984	Cantell's Bt Yd, Newhaven (rlvd by ON.1003)
27.3.1984-31.3.1985	Newhaven (sl)
31.3.1985-16.4.1985	Cantell's Bt Yd, Newhaven (rlvd by ON.1002)
16.4.1985-9.8.1985	Newhaven (sl)
9.8.1985-3.9.1985	Newhaven (ER, new lifeboat ON.1106 on station)
3.9.1985-17.1.1986	Cantell's Bt Yd, Newhaven (std, ER)
17.1.1986-5.5.1986	Ramsgate (rlvg ON.1042: 6/2)
5.5.1986-9.5.1986	Passage to Beaumaris
9.5.1986-9.10.1986	Anglesey Bt Yd, Beaumaris (S, std)
9.10.1986-12.10.1986	Passage to Poole (CT)
12.10.1986-17.10.1986	RNLI Depot, Poole (T)
17.10.1986-20.10.1986	Extended passage to Alderney (CT)
20.10.1986-23.10.1986	Alderney (CT)
23.10.1986-3.11.1987	Alderney (sl, on service at 2215hrs)
3.11.1987-10.12.1987	South Pier Bt Yd, St Helier (rlvd by ON.1003)
10.12.1987-15.12.1988	Alderney (sl)
15.12.1988-2.2.1989	FBM Marine Ltd, Cowes (rlvd by ON.1002)
2.2.1989-11.4.1989	Alderney (sl)
11.4.1989-4.5.1989	South Pier Bt Yd, St Helier (S, rlvd by ON.1003)
4.5.1989-15.9.1990	Alderney (sl)
15.9.1990-27.10.1990	South Pier Bt Yd, St Helier (rlvd by ON.1003)
27.10.1990-19.10.1991	Alderney (sl)
19.10.1991-30.11.1991	South Pier Bt Yd, St Helier (rlvd by ON.1003)
30.11.1991-26.11.1992	Alderney (sl)
26.11.1992-23.1.1993	South Pier Bt Yd, St Helier (S, rlvd by ON.1003)
23.1.1993-7.6.1993	Alderney (sl)
7.6.1993-7.6.1993	South Pier Bt Yd, St Helier (HC)
7.6.1993-18.10.1993	Alderney (sl)
18.10.1993-18.10.1993	South Pier Bt Yd, St Helier (HC)
18.10.1993-7.3.1994	Alderney (sl)
7.3.1994-8.3.1994	Passage to Poole
8.3.1994-10.3.1994	RNLI Depot, Poole (std)
10.3.1994-14.6.1994	Branksea Marine, Wareham (S)

Louis Marchesi of Round Table moored at Newhaven on 18 September 1977 prior to her Naming Ceremony. (Jeff Morris)

Louis Marchesi of Round Table puts to se at the end of her Naming Ceremony on 18 September 1977. (Jeff Morris)

14.6.1994-1.7.1994	RNLI Depot, Poole (std)
1.7.1994-2.7.1994	Passage (via Brixham)
2.7.1994-6.10.1994	Exmouth (sl)
6.10.1994-6.10.1994	Dartside Marine, Dartmouth (HC)
6.10.1994-10.10.1994	Exmouth (sl)
10.10.1994-10.10.1994	Dartside Marine, Dartmouth (HC)
10.10.1994-2.5.1995	Exmouth (sl)
2.5.1995-2.5.1995	Dartside Marine, Dartmouth (HC)
2.5.1995-30.5.1995	Exmouth (sl)
30.5.1995-1.6.1995	Passage to Branksea Marine
1.6.1995-15.8.1995	Branksea Marine, Wareham (S, rlvd by 44-001)
15.8.1995-2.9.1995	RNLI Depot, Poole (T)
2.9.1995-10.7.1996	Exmouth (sl)
10.7.1996-5.12.1996	Souter Sh Yd, Cowes (S)
5.12.1996-20.4.1997	RNLI Depot, Poole (ER)
20.4.1997-22.4.1997	Passage to Courtmacsherry (via Salcombe and Newlyn)
22.4.1997-26.5.1997	Courtmacsherry Harbour (rlvg ON.1205)
26.5.1997-29.5.1997	Passage to Poole (via Newlyn 27-28.5.97 and Salcombe 28.5.97)
29.5.1997-27.7.1998	RNLI Depot, Poole (std)
27.7.1998-28.7.1998	Passage to Falmouth (via Salcombe)
28.7.1998-9.8.1998	Falmouth ("Lifeboats Through the Ages" manned by Falmouth Lifeboat Station 1-9.8.1998)
9.8.1998-10.8.1998	Passage to RNLI Depot, Poole (via Weymouth)
10.8.1998-12.2.1999	RNLI Depot, Poole (std)
12.2.1999-16.2.1999	Passage to Tilbury (via Newhaven 13.2.99, Ramsgate 14.2.99, Sheerness 15.2.99)
16.2.1999	Tilbury (lifted ashore, awaiting shipment to New Zealand)

Notable rescues

On 21 January 1980, the cargo vessel *Athina B*, of Greece, got into difficulties off Brighton Marina. The Shoreham Harbour lifeboat succeeded in rescuing the vessel's crew of 26, for which Coxswain Ken Voice was awarded the Silver medal. *Louis Marchesi of Round Table* also launched to assist, leaving Newhaven under the command of Coxswain/Mechanic Len Patten at 8.50pm. In the exceptionally violent seas being whipped up by the force 9 gale, Coxswain Patten was forced to reduce speed to 10 knots.

During the passage to the casualty in the dark, the lifeboat was twice struck by enormous waves, the second of which caused a 'knock down'. She was laid over on her beam-ends, the wheelhouse was flooded and the capsize switches operated. These switches are automatically triggered when the lifeboat heels over beyond 120 degrees from the vertical and leave the engines idling in neutral. The lifeboat quickly righted herself, the engines were engaged and course was set westward. After covering a further 3 miles in the mountainous seas, a message was received that everyone on board *Athina B* had been rescued so *Louis Marchesi of Round Table* headed back for Newhaven. Although no service had been performed on this occasion, the Waveney design had been tested to the limit.

The other notable service performed by *Louis Marchesi of Round Table* at Newhaven took place in December 1982. At 9.10pm on 9 December, she was launched from Newhaven to stand by the cargo vessel *Andoni*, of Panama, which had broken down in a severe gale, gusting to force 11. The Newhaven tug *Meeching* also put to sea to assist, as did the Shoreham Harbour lifeboat. The two lifeboats stood by as the tug attempted to get a line to the casualty and tow her to safety. The Newhaven lifeboat stood by until 1.55am on 10 December, by which time the tug had towed the coaster 3 miles out to sea. For this service, a Letter of Appreciation was sent to the Master of the tug *Meeching*, and another Letter of Appreciation sent to Coxswain/Mechanic Len Patten and the lifeboat crew.

Disposal

Louis Marchesi of Round Table was placed on the sale list on 29 May 1997 and sold out of service on 12 February 1999 to the Royal New Zealand Coastguard for use as a Rescue Boat based at Waiheke, near Aukland, operated by Waiheke Volunteer Coastguard, New Zealand. She left Tilbury in late February 1999, arrived in New Zealand in April, and was subsequently renamed *P&O Nedlloyd Rescue*.

Above **Leaving the Dock at Exmouth in October 1994,** *Louis Marchesi of Round Table* **was stationed here for two years before being replaced by a 14m Trent. (Nicholas Leach)**

Below *Louis Marchesi of Round Table* **out of the water at Souter's Shipyard, Cowes, in July 1996. (Nicholas Leach)**

Key information

Official Number	1060
Year built	1980
Builder	Fairey Marine
Yard No.	FM 687
Cost	£260,000
Weight	18t16

Donor

Gifts of Mrs Dorothy E Fison, in memory of her husband, and Mrs Knowles; legacy of Mrs Sutcliffe; and a gift from Fisons Ltd.
Named on 26 July 1980 at the Trinity House Pier, Harwich, by Dorothy Fison in memory of her husband.

Stations	Years on station	Record
Harwich	11 Mar 1980 – 6 Oct 1996	232/97
Relief	6 Oct 1996 – 24 Aug 1999	25/3

Movements

10.3.1980-4.8.1981	Harwich (sl)
4.8.1981-8.10.1981	Brooke Marine, Lowestoft (rlvd by ON.1003)
8.10.1981-10.7.1985	Harwich (sl)
10.7.1985-4.11.1985	Crescent Marine, Otterham Quay (rlvd by 44-001)
4.11.1985-10.4.1987	Harwich (sl)
10.4.1987-19.7.1987	Crescent Marine, Otterham Quay (rlvd by ON.1002)
19.7.1987-5.2.1989	Harwich (sl)
5.2.1989-30.4.1989	Crescent Marine, Otterham Quay (S, rlvd by ON.1002)
30.4.1989-30.4.1990	Harwich (sl)
30.4.1990-1.5.1990	Passage to Otterham Quay
1.5.1990-29.6.1990	Crescent Marine, Otterham Quay (S, rlvd by ON.1002)
29.6.1990-29.6.1991	Harwich (sl)
29.6.1991-12.9.1991	Crescent Marine, Otterham Quay (S, rlvd by ON.1002)
12.9.1991-21.10.1992	Harwich (sl)
21.10.1992-5.12.1992	Crescent Marine, Otterham Quay (S, rlvd by ON.1002)
5.12.1992-10.1.1994	Harwich (sl)
10.1.1994-16.3.1994	Crescent Marine, Otterham Quay (S, rlvd by ON.1002)
16.3.1994-5.3.1994	Harwich (sl)
5.3.1995-6.3.1995	Passage (via Sheerness)
6.3.1995-2.5.1995	Crescent Marine, Otterham Quay (S, rlvd by ON.1002)
2.5.1995-6.5.1995	Passage (via Sheerness)
6.5.1995-6.10.1996	Harwich (sl)
6.10.1996-10.10.1996	Passage to Otterham Quay
10.10.1996-4.7.1997	Denton Shiprepairers Ltd, Otterham Quay (S, std)
4.7.1997-7.7.1997	No.4 berth, Sheerness (std)
7.7.1997-10.7.1997	Sheerness (R)
10.7.1997-21.10.1997	Langney Marine, Eastbourne (R, ER)
21.10.1997-22.10.1997	Passage to Lowestoft (via Ramsgate)
22.10.1997-7.11.1998	Lowestoft (rlvg ON.1132)
7.11.1998-8.12.1998	Lowestoft (std)
8.12.1998-10.12.1998	Passage to RNLI Depot, Poole (via Ramsgate 8.12.98 and Newhaven 9.12.98)
10.12.1998-24.8.1999	RNLI Depot, Poole (std, ER)
24.8.1999-25.8.1999	Passage to Tilbury (via Harwich)
25.8.1999-1.9.1999	Harwich (std)
1.9.1999	Tilbury (for shipping to New Zealand)

Notable rescue

On 19 December 1982, the ro-ro ferry *European Gateway* was in collision with the ferry *Speedlink Vanguard* off Felixstowe in near gale force 7, gusting to force 8. Pilot vessels from Harwich were quickly on the scene, and helped to take survivors off the *European Gateway* which had a heavy and increasing list to starboard. *Speedlink Vanguard* was hove-to north-east of the collision position and required no immediate assistance.

John Fison left her moorings at Harwich at 11pm under the command of Coxswain/Mechanic Peter Burwood. The lifeboat reached the scene at 11.28pm by when many of the survivors had been taken off by the pilot vessels and

The scene at Harwich during the Naming Ceremony of *John Fison* on 26 July 1980. (Jeff Morris)

Dressed overall, *John Fison* at Harwich on 26 July 1980 for her formal Naming Ceremony. (Jeff Morris)

transferred to the ferry *Dana Futura*, which was acting as 'on-scene commander'. The lifeboat, searching down tide from the ferry, picked up two men from the water, neither of whom were conscious. Despite the crew's efforts to revive them neither man responded. Meanwhile, the lifeboat continued her search.

At 1.15am on 20 December, *John Fison* assisted one of the pilot vessels to recover a man from the water, and the lifeboat landed three bodies at Harwich before rejoining the search at 1.50am. Five tugs were also on the scene by this time, and they helped to take 18 survivors off the sinking ferry. By 2.30am all but one of the *European Gateway's* complement of 69 had been accounted for, and the various SAR units were gradually stood down.

Framed letters of thanks, signed by the RNLI Chairman, the Duke of Atholl, were presented to Coxswain/Mechanic Burwood, and the Harwich lifeboat crew, Second Coxswain Leslie Smith, Emergency Mechanic Robert Ramplin, and crew members Peter Brand and Peter Dawson. A Bronze medal was awarded to the Coxswain and crew of the Trinity House pilot vessel *Valour* for their efforts during the rescue operation, and letters of appreciation were also sent to others involved in what was a complex rescue operation.

Disposal

John Fison was placed on the sale list on 10 December 1998 and sold out of service on 24 August 1999 to the Royal New Zealand Coastguard for use as a Coastguard Rescue Boat. She left Tilbury Docks on 5 September 1999 and was transported on board the container ship *NZ Pacific* to Wellington, New Zealand, where she was unloaded on 22 October 1999. The engines were started, firing first time, and she was then steamed to Mana, some 6 hours round the coast, where she was lifted out of the water, cleaned and anti-fouled. After being put back into the water she was taken to her new station at Raglan, via New Plymouth, on a 23-hour passage. Renamed *Rotary Rescue,* she is now operated by the Volunteer Coastguard, is ideal for the sea conditions encountered on this part of New Zealand's coastline, and is kept moored just off the Main Raglan Wharf. Funding has come from grants from New Zealand National "Loto" grants board, grant applications to local bodies and trusts, and from the Royal New Zealand Coastguard Federation for some maintenance items and capital expenditure. The Volunteer Coastguard also organise fund-raising activities including a large Golf tournament and fishing contests.

Top   **When first on station at Harwich, *John Fison* was kept at moorings in The Pound. (Nicholas Leach)**

Upper middle   **John Fison at moorings in the Navyard Wharf at Harwich in 1995. (Nicholas Leach)**

Lower middle   **On relief duty at Lowestoft in March 1998, *John Fison* leaves the harbour on exercise. (Nicholas Leach)**

Bottom   **After service *John Fison* was taken to New Zealand for service with the Raglan Volunteer Coastguard. She is seen out of the water being made ready for service prior to being renamed *Rotary Rescue* and entering service. (John Gower)**

Key information

Official Number	1065
Year built	1980
Builder	Fairey Marine
Yard No.	FM 694
Cost	£260,000
Weight	18t9

Donor

Legacies of Mr Colin A S Stringer, Walton-on-Thames, and Mrs A Geraldine Miles, Southbourne, Emsworth. Named to commemorate those who lost their lives in HMS *Barham* in 1941.
Named 17 September 1980 at Gorleston-on-Sea by Mrs Angela Guillaume.

Stations

	Years on station	Record
Gt Yarmouth and Gorleston	30 May 1980 – Mar 1996	254/71
Relief	Apr 1996 – 1999	25/11

Movements

5.5.1980-10.10.1981	Great Yarmouth & Gorleston (sl)
10.10.1981-19.1.1982	Crescent Marine, Otterham Quay (rlvd by ON.1003)
19.1.1982-1.11.1983	Great Yarmouth & Gorleston (sl)
1.11.1983-5.3.1984	Crescent Marine, Otterham Qy (S)
5.3.1984-4.11.1985	Great Yarmouth & Gorleston (sl)
4.11.1985-11.4.1986	Crescent Marine, Otterham Quay (S, rlvd by ON.1002)
11.4.1986-21.7.1987	Great Yarmouth & Gorleston (sl)
21.7.1987-19.3.1988	Crescent Marine, Otterham Quay (S, rlvd by ON.1002)
19.3.1988-28.2.1989	Great Yarmouth & Gorleston (sl)
28.2.1989-3.3.1989	Local Bt Yd (engine repairs)
3.3.1989-6.5.1989	Great Yarmouth & Gorleston (sl)
6.5.1989-7.5.1989	Passage to Rochester
7.5.1989-15.7.1989	Crescent Marine, Otterham Quay (S, rlvd by ON.1002)
15.7.1989-9.7.1990	Great Yarmouth & Gorleston (sl)
9.7.1990-20.10.1990	Crescent Mar, Otterham Quay (S)
20.10.1990-16.9.1991	Great Yarmouth & Gorleston (sl)
16.9.1991-15.2.1992	Crescent Mar, Otterham Quay (S, rlvd by ON.1002)
15.2.1992-14.2.1993	Great Yarmouth & Gorleston (sl)
14.2.1993-9.4.1993	Fletchers Bt Yd, Lowestoft (S, rlvd by ON.1002)
9.4.1993-13.5.1993	Great Yarmouth & Gorleston (sl)
13.5.1993-14.5.1993	Fletchers Bt Yd, Lowestoft (HC)
14.5.1993-13.1.1994	Great Yarmouth & Gorleston (sl)
13.1.1994-13.1.1994	Fletchers Bt Yd, Lowestoft (HC)
13.1.1994-4.4.1994	Great Yarmouth & Gorleston (sl)
4.4.1994-17.6.1994	Fletchers Bt Yd, Lowestoft (rlvd by ON.1002)
17.6.1994-24.8.1994	Great Yarmouth & Gorleston (sl)
24.8.1994-29.9.1994	Goodchild Marine, Burgh castle (R)
29.9.1994-22.3.1995	Great Yarmouth & Gorleston (sl)
22.3.1995-22.3.1995	Fletchers Bt Yd, Lowestoft (HC)
22.3.1995-23.3.1995	Great Yarmouth & Gorleston (sl)
23.3.1995-23.3.1995	Goodchild Marine, Burgh castle (R)
23.3.1995-11.5.1995	Great Yarmouth & Gorleston (sl)
11.5.1995-1.8.1995	Fletchers Bt Yd, Lowestoft (S, rlvd by ON.1002)
1.8.1995-6.12.1995	Great Yarmouth & Gorleston (sl)
6.12.1995-6.12.1995	Fletchers Bt Yd, Lowestoft (R)
6.12.1995-25.2.1996	Great Yarmouth & Gorleston (sl)
25.2.1996-26.2.1996	Passage at Sheerness
26.2.1996-2.6.1996	Denton Shiprepairers Ltd, Otterham Quay (std, ER)
2.6.1996-5.6.1996	Passage to Dunmore East (via Newhaven 2.6.96, Weymouth 3.6.96, Newlyn 4.6.96)
5.6.1996-8.10.1996	Dunmore East (rlvg ON.1035)
8.10.1996-17.10.1996	Passage to Sheerness (via Kilmore Quay)
17.10.1996-19.10.1996	Passage to Otterham Quay (via Newlyn 17.10.96, Salcombe 18.10.96)
19.10.1996-25.10.1996	RNLI Depot, Poole (awaiting passage to Otterham Quay)
25.10.1996-26.10.1996	Passage to Otterham Quay
26.10.1996-30.10.1996	Passage to Dentons Shiprepairers Ltd (via Sheerness)
30.10.1996-6.4.1997	Denton Shiprepairers Ltd, Otterham

After her Naming Ceremony on 17 September 1980, *Barham* puts to sea for a short demonstration. (Jeff Morris)

***Barham* shows her speed after the Ceremony, with Lowestoft lifeboat *Frederick Edward Crick* in attendance. (Jeff Morris)**

	Quay (S, std)
6.4.1997-20.4.1997	Walton & Frinton (rlvg ON.1154)
20.4.1997-21.4.1997	Sheerness (std, awaiting passage)
21.4.1997-5.6.1997	Denton Shiprepairers Ltd, Otterham Quay (std, ER)
5.6.1997-16.6.1997	Passage to Eastbourne
16.6.1997-11.11.1997	Langney Mar, Eastbourne (std, ER)
11.11.1997-12.11.1997	Passage to St Helier (via Yarmouth)
12.11.1997-1.12.1998	St Helier (relieveing ON.1157)
1.12.1998-17.1.1999	St Helier (awaiting passage)
17.1.1999-18.1.1999	Passage to Poole (via Alderney)
18.1.1999-28.11.1999	RNLI Depot, Poole (std)
28.11.1999-29.11.1999	Final passage prior to shipping (via Newhaven)
29.11.1999	Sheerness (std, prior to shipping)

Notable rescues

In the early hours of 3 May 1982 the yacht *Seamist* ran aground on the Scroby Sands in rough seas, and after the wind strengthened to gale force her crew of two radioed the coastguard for help. *Barham* left her moorings at Gorleston at 2.49am and headed out into very rough seas. Almost an hour later the yacht was found 2 miles north-north-west of the Cross Sands Buoy.

With Coxswain/Mechanic Richard Hawkins at the helm, the lifeboat circled the casualty, which was rolling violently making an approach alongside hazardous. Therefore, an attempt was made to get a tow line on board, but the two yachtsmen were too exhausted by this time to secure it. Therefore, Coxswain/Mechanic Hawkins had to take the lifeboat as close as he could to enable lifeboatman Paul Carter to be transferred to the yacht.

With one of the lifeboatmen on board, the tow line was then successfully secured and the tow got underway at 4.45am. It lasted for almost three hours, and it was not until 7.30am that the two boats entered Gorleston harbour. For this rescue, the Thanks on Vellum was accorded to Coxswain/Mechanic Hawkins. A framed letter of thanks, signed by the RNLI Chairman The Duke of Atholl, was presented to lifeboatman Paul Carter.

The second notable service performed by *Barham* while she was stationed at Great Yarmouth & Gorleston began at 11.35pm on 19 August 1990 when she was launched to go to an injured man on board the yacht *Southern Cross*. By the time the lifeboat reached the casualty, at 1.10am on 20 August, 6 miles from the Smiths Knoll Lightvessel, the wind had increased to near gale force.

Despite heavy rain reducing visibility, Coxswain/Mechanic Hawkins twice attempted to take the lifeboat alongside the yacht, but in seas 10ft high had to pull back because of the yacht's violent motion. On the third attempt, Second Coxswain David Mason managed to board the yacht and found the skipper very weak and unsteady. It then took another six attempts to get the lifeboat alongside before the skipper was safely transferred from the yacht.

A helicopter was then summoned and at 1.50am lifted the man off the lifeboat and flew him to hospital. The yacht was then taken in tow and brought into Gorleston harbour, which was reached at 5.15am. For this rescue, the Thanks on Vellum was accorded to Coxswain/Mechanic Hawkins. A

framed Letter of Thanks signed by the RNLI Chairman was presented to Second Coxswain Mason.

Disposal

Barham was placed on the sale list on 18 January 1999 and sold out of service in 1999 to the Royal New Zealand Coastguard and became a lifeboat at Napier, Hawke Bay.

Top **On routine exercise, *Barham* leaves Gorleston harbour in a moderate swell. (John Markham)**

Middle **The mooring pen constructed at Gorleston in 1993 was designed for the 14m Trent lifeboat, but was used by *Barham* until the Trent arrived. (Nicholas Leach)**

Bottom **Barham leaving Gorleston harbour on exercise in September 1995. (Nicholas Leach)**

Key information

Official Number	1079
Year built	1982
Builder	Fairey Marine
Yard No.	FM 710
Cost	£319,940
Weight	18t18

Donor

Legacies of Miss Mabel Hewson, Mrs Mary Grey, Mrs Rhoda Whittaker, Mr L G A Dunn and Mr Frank Rowe. Named on 17 September 1983 at Dun Cow Quay, Blyth, by the Duchess of Northumberland, after parents of the donor, Miss Hewson.

Stations

Station	Years on station	Record
Blyth	26 Oct 1982 – Dec 1995	136/43
Larne	19 Mar 1996 – Nov 1998	23/11

Movements

1.10.1982-29.3.1984	Blyth (sl)
29.3.1984-2.5.1984	Robson's Bt Yd, South Shields (S)
2.5.1984-25.7.1985	Blyth (sl)
25.7.1985-15.10.1985	Robson's Bt Yd, South Shields (M)
15.10.1985-19.2.1987	Blyth (sl)
19.2.1987-6.4.1987	Amble Bt Co, Amble (S, rlvd by ON.1043)
6.4.1987-10.4.1987	Amble Bt Co, Amble (T)
10.4.1987-3.5.1987	Blyth (sl)
3.5.1987-4.5.1987	Blyth (M)
4.5.1987-1.6.1987	Blyth (sl)
1.6.1987-1.6.1987	Blyth (M)
1.6.1987-18.1.1988	Blyth (sl)
18.1.1988-4.3.1988	Amble Bt Co, Amble (S, rlvd by ON.1043)
4.3.1988-10.3.1988	Amble Bt Co, Amble (T)
10.3.1988-3.5.1989	Blyth (sl)
3.5.1989-23.6.1989	Robson's Bt Yd, South Shields (S, rlvd by ON.1043)
23.6.1989-11.10.1990	Blyth (sl)
11.10.1990-14.12.1990	Amble Bt Co, Amble (S, rlvd by ON.1034)
14.12.1990-6.1.1992	Blyth (sl)
6.1.1992-22.2.1992	Amble Bt Co, Amble (S, rlvd by ON.1001)
22.2.1992-18.4.1993	Blyth (sl)
18.4.1993-4.6.1993	Amble Bt Co, Amble (S, rlvd by ON.1001)
4.6.1993-12.6.1994	Blyth (sl)
12.6.1994-10.8.1994	Amble Bt Co, Amble (rlvd by ON.1001)
10.8.1994-10.9.1995	Blyth (sl)
10.9.1995-9.12.1995	Amble Bt Co, Amble (S, rlvd by ON.1001)
9.12.1995-13.12.1995	Passage to Poole (via Scarborough 9-10.12.95, Ramsgate 11.12.95, Newhaven 12.12.95)
13.12.1995-12.1.1996	RNLI Depot, Poole
12.1.1996-19.1.1996	Passage to Larne to establish new station (via Brixham 12.1.96, Fowey 13.1.96, Newlyn 14.1.96, Fishguard 15.1.96, Wicklow 16.1.96, Port St Mary 17.1.96, Bangor, NI, 18.1.96)
19.1.1996-10.2.1996	Larne (CT)
10.2.1996-16.2.1996	Bangor NI (CT, R)
16.2.1996-24.2.1996	Larne (CT)
24.2.1996-25.2.1996	Passage to Campbeltown (CT)
25.2.1996-23.7.1996	Larne (CT)
23.7.1996-23.7.1996	Bangor Shipyard, NI (HC)
23.7.1996-6.4.1997	Larne (sl)
6.4.1997-22.6.1997	Survey (rlvd by ON.1042)
22.6.1997-25.9.1997	Larne (sl)
25.9.1997-25.9.1997	Bangor Marina (HC)
25.9.1997-8.4.1998	Larne (sl)
8.4.1998-8.4.1998	Bangor Marina (HC)
8.4.1998-11.11.1998	Larne (sl)
11.11.1998-20.11.1998	Larne (std, awaiting move to Poole)
20.11.1998-26.11.1998	Passage to RNLI Depot, Poole (via Bangor 21.11.98, Dun Laoghaire 22.11.98, Dunmore East 23.11.98,

The William and Jane at Dun Cow Quay, Blyth, for her Naming Ceremony on 17 September 1983. (Jeff Morris)

The champagne bottle breaks over the bow of *The William and Jane* at the end of her Naming Ceremony. (Jeff Morris)

	Newlyn 24.11.98, Salcombe 25.11.98)
26.11.1998-22.5.1999	RNLI Depot, Poole (on sale list)
22.5.1999-25.5.1999	Passage to Tilbury (via Souter Sh Yd, Cowes 22.5.99, Langney Marine, Eastbourne 23.5.99, and Sheerness 24.5.99)
25.5.1999	Tilbury (for shipping to New Zealand)

Notable rescue

On 7 December 1982 *The William and Jane* was launched from Blyth under Coxswain Charles Hatcher to the fishing vessel *Castle Cove*, which was taking water 5 miles off the Tyne. The wind, near gale force 7, was blowing from the east, and the lifeboat encountered heavy breaking seas as she left harbour. During the passage the lifeboat was continually washed by breaking seas, reaching the casualty at 7pm

Because its crew of three did not want to abandon their vessel, a tow rope was passed. With breaking seas 15 to 20 feet high, the tow towards the Tyne began at quarter speed. The fishing vessel's engines had broken down and water in her hull made her unstable. The 5 mile tow took over an hour, and at 8.34pm the two craft approached the Tyne.

As they were about to enter the river, the fishing vessel began to sink. The tow line was therefore quickly slipped and retrieved on board *The William and Jane*. The lifeboat then came alongside the sinking vessel, which had heeled over to starboard. The three fishermen slid down the port side of the heavily rolling boat and were pulled aboard by the lifeboat's crew. The fishermen were then landed at Tyne Fish Quay and the lifeboat returned to Blyth.

For this rescue, Coxswain Hatcher was awarded the Bronze medal and medal service certificates were presented to the remainder of the crew, Second Coxswain Thomas Moss, Mechanic John Scott, Assistant Mechanic Dallas Taylor, Emergency Mechanic Keith Barnard and crew member Ian Woodhouse.

Disposal

The William and Jane was placed on the sale list on 26 November 1998 and sold out of service in May 1999 to the Royal New Zealand Coastguard Federation. Renamed *John Barton Acland Rescue,* she is now a Rescue Boat based at Kaikoura, on South Island, 180km north of Christchurch.

Top   **The William and Jane returning from exercise at Blyth in September 1991. (Brian Chandler)**

Upper middle   **The first all-weather lifeboat at Larne, *The William and Jane* seen underway in Larne Lough. (From a photo supplied by Paddy McLaughlin)**

Lower middle   **After being taken out of service, *The William and Jane* was stored at RNLI Depot, Poole, in February 1999. (Nicholas Leach)**

Bottom   **After service, *The William and Jane* seen in her NZ Coastguard colours, moored at Kaikoura and renamed *John Barton Acland Rescue*. (Richard Craig)**

After service summary

Op No	ON	Station	Replacement	Sold	Renamed	Current location
44-001		Relief	—	—	44-001	Chatham Dockyard
44-002	1001	Dun Laoghaire	Waveney 44-015	1996	*Sarah JFK*	Davy Bank, Newcastle
44-003	1002	Gorleston	Waveney 44-021	1999	*P&O Nedlloyd Stratheden*	Botany Bay, Australia
44-004	1003	Dover Holyhead	50ft Thames 47ft Tyne	1999	*P&O Nedlloyd Strathmore*	Narooma, Australia
44-005	1004	Amble Harwich	12m Mersey Waveney 44-020	1999	*St Hilda of Whitby*	Whitby, North Yorkshire
44-006	1005	Barry Dock Donaghadee Courtmacsherry	52ft Arun 52ft Arun 14m Trent	1999	*P&O Nedlloyd Strathallan*	Ulladulla, Australia
44-007	1006	Troon Arklow	Waveney 44-011 Waveney 44-011	1999	*P&O Nedlloyd Rawalpindi*	Sydney, Australia
44-008	1026	Eyemouth	14m Trent	2000		Namibia
44-009	1027	Sheerness Achill	14m Trent 52ft Arun	1998	*Badger*	Port St Mary, Isle of Man
44-010	1028	Plymouth Fowey	52ft Arun 14m Trent	1999	*Westgate Rescue*	New Plymouth, N Zealand
44-011	1029	Poole Troon Arklow	33ft Brede 52ft Arun 14m Trent	1999	*P&O Nedlloyd Strathaird*	Broken Bay, Australia
44-012	1033	Whitby Invergordon	47ft Tyne 14m Trent	1999	*IA.001*	Roberts Bank, Canada
44-013	1034	St Helier Dunbar	47ft Tyne 14m Trent	1998	*North Esk*	Montrose, Aberdeenshire
44-014	1035	Dunmore East	14m Trent	1999	*P&O Nedlloyd Strathnaver*	Batemans Bay, Australia
44-015	1036	Fleetwood Dun Laoghaire	47ft Tyne 14m Trent	1996	*St Boisel*	Berwick, Northumberland
44-016	1042	Ramsgate Tobermory Portree	47ft Tyne 54ft Arun 14m Trent	1998	*West Swann*	Port Howard, Falkland Is
44-017	1043	Donaghadee Sunderland	Waveney 44-006 14m Trent	1999	*Trust Porirua Rescue*	Mana, New Zealand
44-018	1044	Hartlepool	47ft Tyne	1997	*ADES 16 14-016*	Montevideo, Uruguay
44-019	1045	Exmouth Alderney Newhaven	14m Trent 14m Trent 52ft Arun	1999	*P&O Nedlloyd Rescue*	Waiheke Island, N Zealand
44-020	1060	Harwich	17m Severn	1999	*Rotary Rescue*	Raglan, New Zealand
44-021	1065	Gorleston	14m Trent	1999		Napier, New Zealand
44-022	1079	Blyth Larne	14m Trent 52ft Arun	1999	*John Barton Acland Rescue*	Kaikoura, New Zealand

Portree
Invergorden
Tobermory
Dunbar
Eyemouth
Larne
Amble
Troon
Blyth
Sunderland
Achill Island
Donaghadee
Hartlepool
Whitby
Fleetwood
Holyhead
Gt. Yarmouth & Gorleston
Dun Laoghaire
Arklow
Harwich
Barry Dock
Sheerness
Dunmore East
Ramsgate
Courtmacsherry Harbour
Exmouth
Poole
Dover
Newhaven
Fowey
Plymouth

● St. Helier, Jersey

● Alderney

Note: This map does not show stations at which Waveneys served only as a Relief lifeboat.

Opposite Seen after being withdrawn from Gorleston, *Barham* (ON.1065) stored at Langney Marine, Eastbourne, in July 1997. (Nick Hall)